Nine Essential

BLUE JOURNAL ARTICLES

View Legal

Matthew Burgess

Patrick Ellwood

NINE ESSENTIAL BLUE JOURNAL ARTICLES

National Library of Australia Cataloguing-in-Publication entry: (paperback)

Author: Burgess, Matthew, author.
Title: The nine essential blue journal articles / Matthew Burgess;
and Patrick Ellwood
interior book layout by Otto Dimitrijevics.
Edition: 3rd edition.
ISBN: 9781925181555 (paperback)
Subjects: Estate planning—Australia.
Trusts and trustees—Australia.
Executors and administrators—Australia.
Probate law and practice—Australia.
Other Authors/Contributors: Ellwood, Patrick, author
Dewey Number: 332.0240160994

Important disclaimer

This book covers legal and technical issues in a general way. It is not designed to express opinions on specific cases. This book is intended for information purposes only and should not be regarded as legal advice. Further advice should be obtained before taking action on any issue dealt with in this publication.

CONTENTS

The use of special purpose trusts in estate planning – part 1 9

The use of special purpose trusts in estate planning – part 2 33

Trust assets and estate planning: how has the dust settled after Kennon v Spry? 53

Failed trust distributions: their tax consequences 97

Fixed trusts and unit trusts: one and the same? 131

Testamentary trusts: bespoke planning opportunities 169

The Clark decision: possible consequences for CGT event E4? 211

Bust proofing trusts 219

Insurance funded business succession 253

About the authors

Matthew Burgess, Patrick Ellwood, Naomi Arnold and Tara Lucke are co-founders, of View Legal.

Having previously founded Australia's first virtual law firm as a wholly owned subsidiary of one of the country's leading independent law firms, View Legal is results focused and passionate about delivering new solutions in a way that aligns with their 'SPS'–service and price satisfaction–guarantee.

As authors, Patrick and Matthew are recognised as experts in their fields, who constantly create innovative strategies for the growth, management and protection of wealth.

They are published across a range of topics including:

1. The Nine Steps to a Complete Estate Plan.
2. The Five Foundations of Business Succession.
3. The Seven key aspects of Testamentary Trusts.
4. Inside Stories–the complete collection of blog posts (2010-2014)
5. The Seven Key Aspects of SMSFs.

THE USE OF SPECIAL PURPOSE TRUSTS IN ESTATE PLANNING – PART 1

The use of special purpose trusts in estate planning – part 1

IN LIGHT OF fundamental changes to the taxation regime and the expanding wealth of Australia's aging population, there is a growing need for estate planning to utilise appropriate structuring. This article focuses on the use of special purpose trusts in the estate planning process.

Introduction

In recent years, the need for effective structuring of business and personal assets has been brought into sharp focus for high net worth individuals and business owners.

Fundamental changes to the taxation regime, the vast amounts of wealth accumulated within superannuation funds and the increasing tendency for both business and personal relationships to be relatively short term, as opposed to life long, have meant that traditional estate planning has been revolutionised.

A significant factor to note in the changing face of estate planning is the transfer of wealth from Australia's 'baby boomer' generation. Statistically, this segment of the population is by far the wealthiest and best educated in Australia's history, and consequently far more sophisticated estate planning strategies are being developed in order to minimise the ability for wealth to be attacked by creditors, former spouses, business associates and (in some instances) disgruntled beneficiaries.

While tax effective strategies incorporating complex will arrangements and testamentary trusts continue to be of relevance, recent developments in estate planning have been more focused on the protection of underlying wealth.

In particular, additional structures are now being utilised in conjunction with wills to ensure wealth passes efficiently to the intended recipients and that the transfer takes place at the intended time. Often the desire to ensure a suitable tax outcome needs to be balanced against a desire to ensure assets are protected from family disputes, spendthrift beneficiaries and creditors in deciding on an estate plan.

Asset protection strategies and the use of special purpose trusts are important issues to consider in estate planning, particularly where potential beneficiaries are in occupations, professional practice or in business, or where there is a risk that a personal relationship of a beneficiary may degenerate in the future. Potential beneficiaries that fall into any of these 'at risk' categories will be exposed to losing assets, unless appropriate structures are put in place.

The difficulty in many estate planning exercises is that serious attempts to devise and implement a plan are often not made until some 'triggering event' stimulates action. Often the triggering event is itself an issue that may jeopardise the ability to implement appropriate strategies, for example financial or matrimonial misfortune or life threatening illness.

Given that the first wave of the baby boomer generation is now nearing 60, it is likely that the increased importance placed in recent years on appropriately structuring intergenerational wealth transfers will continue to intensify.

There are an enormous number of aspects to a comprehensive estate plan. This paper will focus on the use of special purpose trusts in the context of estate planning.

The paper will consider the use of trusts in the following situations:

a passing your estate to wastrel children;
b the use of trusts and family law;
c bankrupt or at risk beneficiaries;

d Division 6AA issues and tax; and
e superannuation and death benefits.

Each of the above issues are dealt with in turn below.

Wastrel children

In the event that it is necessary to protect an estate from wastrel children or likewise spendthrift children testamentary trusts and estate proceeds trusts can be useful. The structure of each of these two trusts and the advantages and disadvantages are outlined below.

Testamentary trusts

Testamentary trusts are simply trusts established pursuant to a will. In recent years numerous different types of testamentary trusts have included fixed, unit, discretionary (family), hybrid, resulting (constructive), bare, lineal descendent and superannuation proceeds trusts. The various types of trusts have a number of different features and specific uses, but fundamentally the legal structure of all testamentary trusts are very similar.

Structure of testamentary trusts

Essentially, the share of the estate intended for each beneficiary can be managed via a testamentary trust by the trustee appointed by the testator in their will (often the trustee and a beneficiary of the trust may be the same person although the advantages and disadvantages of this approach are dealt with in more detail below).

During each year the trustees of the trust may have complete discretionary power to choose which beneficiary takes what share of income for that year. They may also have the absolute discretion as to the distribution of capital, but often the distribution of capital can be limited to set amounts and for a limited range of direct descendants, or otherwise as instructed by a testator.

A will maker (or testator) sets out the terms of the trust in their will and can give the trustee complete discretion as to who should receive capital and income from the trust or alternatively the testator can restrict the trustee's discretion as much as they like.

A 'lineal descendant' trust is simply a specific type of testamentary trust whereby the testator may restrict the ability of the trustee so they may only distribute income or capital (or both) to the testator's children and grandchildren and so on, excluding any spouse of the children and/or grandchildren.

The main attraction to excluding spouses as potential beneficiaries is that in the event of a matrimonial (or de facto) relationship breakdown it is unlikely that a lineal descendant trust would be taken into account by the Family Court as anything other than a resource of the relevant marriage. Thus the assets of the testamentary trust are likely to be protected in this scenario.

Conversely, many people argue that the flexibilities normally associated with a trust structure are significantly diminished if a whole class of potential beneficiaries are excluded.

In recent times many people have adopted a 'hybrid' approach to testamentary trusts so that spouses can be potential income beneficiaries from year to year but that in relation to any capital distributions from the trust, these distributions may only be made to lineal descendants of the original will maker.

Advantages of testamentary trusts

The main advantages of an appropriately drafted testamentary discretionary trust ('**TDT**') established by a will are as follows:

a the flexibility given to the trustees to allocate income and capital with reference to the facts at the time, rather than a testator's prediction (no matter how careful) of the future. It allows the trustee to make a greater distribution for a testator's child with a special need, such as (in particular) wastrel children, as well as those with a disability;

b if an estate was left to a child absolutely then it is their property and could be jeopardised by their financial position at the time of death or after. In addition, should that child suffer matrimonial or financial misfortune at some time in the future, the trust at least provides a facility whereby the inheritance can be kept separate. As indicated above, it is unlikely (particularly where spouses are not potential beneficiaries) that the assets of the **TDT** would be seen as anything more than a resource for the relevant beneficiary and not part of the assets of the matrimonial pool which are physically distributed between the parties to the marriage breakdown;

c the TDT can be drafted such that it complies with the requirements set out in s 102AG(2)(a)(i) Income Tax Assessment Act 1936 ('ITAA 1936'), so that income each year allocated to minor children is not subject to the same tax rates as if it were a normal family discretionary trust established during a person's lifetime (where the first $416 distributed to a child is tax-free but then any further income is taxed at the highest rate which could be up to 66 percent);

d where income is derived under the section quoted above infant children are assessed at the normal, individual rates (the first, approximately, $24,000 tax-free and the balance at normal adult rates) which may be a significant saving in tax when you look at the gross income for a family unit. The Commissioner does have some discretion in these cases, but generally the discretion is exercised in favour of the TDTs as they are a 'traditional' form of trust; and

e even if, for any reason the trust does not come into effect through the operation of law, or it fails, then the will can include a fall-back provision whereby the capital vests in the intended beneficiary anyway, with provision for their children if necessary, or even revert to trusts established for other beneficiaries.

Ultimately TDTs are particularly useful structures in the following circumstances:

a. to ensure concessional tax treatment is available to distributions of capital and income to minor beneficiaries;
b. to protect accumulated wealth from wastrel or spendthrift beneficiaries;
c. to provide for infant children and disabled beneficiaries; and
d. to protect inheritances from attack by the family law courts and trustee in bankruptcy.

Disadvantages of testamentary trusts

There are a number of potential disadvantages to TDTs, including:

a. once income is determined to be distributed to an infant and is then not applied in payment of the infant's needs there will be an accumulating debt owing to that infant by the TDT. Thus when it comes time to wind up the trust and for the beneficiaries to take the capital, they may find the capital substantially eroded by the necessity to pay these debts to the children or other beneficiaries, unless of course they are in some way forgiven. Alternatively, when the relevant child reaches the age of majority it may be that they seek repayment of the loan owing to them;
b. the TDT structure requires a reasonable degree of control, similar to a normal family discretionary trust, including recourse to competent accountants and lawyers for trust administration advice. This all involves a cost;
c. the taxation aspects of a TDT have not been ably and forcefully contested in a Court in the last decade. Notwithstanding this, the language of s 102AG(2)(a)(i) of the ITAA 1936 is clear and there are income tax rulings (both private and public rulings) given in favour of the establishment of TDTs; and
d. where the beneficiary of a trust is also a trustee, they should for safety's sake always have at least one trustee with them when undertaking trust related issues, so the beneficiary will need to

be able to work with their co-trustee as protection against creditors or former spouses is diminished when a beneficiary is the sole trustee of the trust, as that beneficiary has power as trustee to distribute the whole of the income and/or capital to themselves. Finding suitable co-trustees can be a difficult exercise, and can also cause increased expenses where a professional is appointed.

Estate proceeds trusts

A proceeds trust can be either an 'estate proceeds' trust (where the proceeds were originally part of the deceased estate), or a non-estate proceeds trust (where the proceeds originate from an asset which does not form part of the deceased estate). Some common examples of non-estate proceeds are superannuation entitlements or life insurance.

An estate proceeds trust is a trust established by a deed after the death of the deceased. It is most commonly used to obtain advantageous income tax treatment for income allocated to minor beneficiaries.

Generally, an estate proceeds trust is more restrictive than an ordinary TDT established pursuant to the terms of a will. An estate proceeds trust differs from an ordinary testamentary trust on account of the following features (s 102AG of ITM 1936):

a minor beneficiaries (persons under 18 years of age on establishment of the trust) must be the ultimate capital beneficiaries of the trust, meaning the assets of the trust must ultimately vest in them;
b the transfer of estate assets to the trust must occur within 3 calendar years of the date of death of the deceased; and
c the assets transferred must not exceed the entitlements that the minor beneficiaries would have received if the deceased had not left a valid will (i.e. if the deceased had died intestate).

The main advantage of an estate proceeds trust other than providing a level of asset protection (particularly for wastrel beneficiaries) is the concessional tax treatment of income distributed from the trust and the ability to split income according to the financial circumstances and needs of the deceased's children.

The income distributed from the trust may be used to pay for the children's education, living and other expenses and any income received by a minor will be taxed at the normal adult rate, rather than the penal rate that normally applies to income distributions to infant children. As noted above, this means that assuming the children are not earning other income they will be eligible for the, approximately, $24,000 tax-free threshold for income received by each child per financial year. Any additional income will be taxed at the ordinary adult marginal rates.

There are a number of technical issues that must always be reviewed before establishing an estate proceeds trust including:

a the concessional rates of tax will generally not be available to the grandchildren of a testator;

b while assets in excess of what the testator's children may have received on an intestacy can be contributed to the estate proceeds trust, only the income generated by that portion of the capital which the testator's children would have received on an intestacy will be entitled to the concessional rates of taxation; and

c any assets that do not form part of the testator's estate such as assets owned as joint tenants with a spouse or insurance policies that are owned by the surviving spouse will not be able to be contributed to the estate proceeds trust.

The use of trusts and family law

Trusts and the Family Law Act

Generally speaking the Family Court only has power to deal with the rights or impose duties on parties who are the subject of the application (in other words the husband and wife personally). This means that the Family Court cannot deal with assets held via a trust structure as they do not form part of the asset pool available for distribution.

There are a number of exceptions to this general rule, including:

a where assets have been transferred to a trust as part of a 'sham' directly designed to defeat an application of a spouse. Generally the Court will only interfere where a transfer of assets to a trust has taken place during or in anticipation of property settlement proceedings and there are no other commercial reasons justifying the transfer;
b if the parties to the relationship have made some sort of nuptial (or financial) agreement in relation to the assets of the trust then the trust can be bound to comply with this agreement; and
c where the family trust is seen as simply the 'alter-ego' or as a 'puppet' of a party to the marriage. This issue revolves mainly around the Court's determination of who controls the trust, and this issue is dealt with in more detail below.

If none of the abovementioned factors apply then the most the Family Court is likely to do in relation to the assets of a trust is to take those assets into account as a 'resource' of the marriage, as opposed to an 'asset'.

Resource / asset distinction

Generally speaking the distinction between a resource and an asset for family law purposes is as follows:

a a resource is property that, while a party to the marriage may have access to, they do not directly own or control it. Therefore while the resource may be taken into account when determining the division of matrimonial assets the property cannot be directly dealt with by the Court;

b an asset is an item of property the interest in which can be allocated by the Court in such ways it determines reasonable.

In order to determine the way in which the assets of a relationship are divided and the extent to which resources are taken into account, the Family Court determines the parties' financial and non-financial contributions to the asset pool and then considers a number of factors which are set out under the *Family Law Act 1975* including:

c the age and state of health of each of the parties;

d the income, property and financial resources of each of the parties and the physical and mental capacity of each of them to obtain appropriate gainful employment;

e whether either party has the care or control of a child of the marriage who has not attained the age of 18 years;

f commitments of each of the parties that are necessary to enable the party to support:
  (i) himself or herself; and
  (ii) a child or another person that the party has a duty to maintain;

g the responsibilities of either party to support any other person;

h the eligibility of either party for a pension, allowance or benefit under:
  (i) any law of the Commonwealth, of a State or Territory or of another country; or
  (ii) any superannuation fund or scheme, whether the fund or scheme was established, or operates, within or outside Australia; and
  (iii) the rate of any such pension, allowance or benefit being paid to either party;

i where the parties have separated or the marriage has been dissolved, the standard of living that in all the circumstances is reasonable;
j the extent to which the payment of maintenance to the party whose maintenance is under consideration would increase the earning capacity of that party by enabling that party to undertake a course of education or training or to establish himself or herself in a business or otherwise to obtain an adequate income;
k the extent to which the party whose maintenance is under consideration has contributed to the income, earning capacity, property and financial resources of the other party;
l the duration of the marriage and the extent to which it has affected the earning capacity of the party whose maintenance is under consideration;
m the need to protect a party who wishes to continue that party's role as a parent;
n if either party is cohabiting with another person, the financial circumstances relating to the cohabitation;
o any child support under the Child Support (Assessment) Act 1989 that a party to the marriage has provided, is to provide, or might be liable to provide in the future, for a child of the marriage;
p any fact or circumstance which, in the opinion of the court, the justice of the case requires to be taken into account; and
q the terms of any financial agreement that is binding on the parties.

Obviously the weighting given to each of the above factors will vary from case to case.

Control of family trust

As indicated, the control of a family trust by one of the parties to the marriage will be a key factor in determining:

a. firstly, whether it will be treated as an asset of a party to the marriage, due to one or more of the factors set out above; and
b. secondly if it is not an asset of the marriage, the extent it will be taken into account as a resource of a party to the marriage.

'Under a lineal descendant trust 'the trustee', may only distribute income or capital (or both) to the testator's children and grandchildren and so on, excluding any spouse of the children'

The determination of the way in which trust property will be dealt with in any particular case is a question of fact. The determination will depend upon the way in which the Court interprets all the relevant circumstances of the particular case. In making this assessment the Court normally has regard to the following aspects of control (in no particular order):

a. the benefits derived from the trust by the parties to the marriage such as loans, salaries and payment of expenses etc;
b. the degree to which a party is able to distribute to themselves all of the income and capital of the trust;
c. the history of the party's treatment of the trust property;
d. the history of distributions made by the trust to the party;
e. the party's past exercise of powers and involvement in variations or amendments to the trust deed;
f. the degree of the party's influence over the trust including the trustee (or directors of the corporate trustee) and the appointor;
g. the ability to direct or otherwise control the trustee;
h. the capacity of a party to borrow on trust funds;
i. the potential for the party to receive the ultimate benefit of the trust property; and
j. whether a party has responsibility for the day-to-day administration of the trust.

The effect of trusts and binding financial agreements on family provision applications

Increasingly there is a focus in any estate planning exercise on preventing a Family Provision Application ('FPA') being brought against an estate by an estranged child or the children of the client's second spouse. It is usually the case that a potential applicant has to establish financial need or show their efforts significantly contributed to the assets of the deceased. Where this is potentially the case, and the will maker is still wanting to minimise that person's entitlement, the will maker will often transfer assets into a family discretionary trust (or other similar entity) such that there are no assets in their estate on their death which can be subject to the FPA.

The effectiveness of such asset protection strategies have come under increasing scrutiny in recent years.

The recent High Court decision of *Barns v Barns* (2003) HCA 9 (where the High Court decided not follow the majority decision of the Privy Council in *Schaefer v Schuhmann* (1972) AC 572 but to follow the Privy Council's judgment in *Dillon v Public Trustee of New Zealand* (1941) AC 294 and the dissenting judgment of Lord Simon in Schaefer) is an example of the Court upholding an applicant's statutory rights in the face of a traditional asset protection strategy (mutual wills) being used in an attempt to frustrate a FPA. The lesson from Barns is to never take anything for granted when dealing with potential FPA applicants and to ensure that all contingencies are properly considered before the effort and expense of transferring assets into a discretionary trust or similar entity.

In the case of *Barns*, Mr Barns entered into a Deed with his wife and son whereby he and his wife agreed not to revoke the wills which were annexed to the Deed, without the written consent of the other parties to that Deed. The mutual wills would firstly leave the estate to the surviving spouse. On the death of the surviving spouse, the estate would then be left to the son. The intention behind the drafting of the Deed and the mutual wills was to prevent the parents' daughter from benefiting or participating in the estate of the surviving parent.

On the death of Mr Barns (the first spouse), his daughter made a successful application for provision under the *Inheritance (Family Provision) Act* 1972 (SA) ('the Act').

Barns case

The key questions in Barns were:

a did the Deed operate to effectively reduce the testator's estate to nil, in that the testator had entered into a contractual arrangement with his wife and son to dispose of his entire estate at death, so there is no estate which can be subject to the FPA?; or
b was the Deed and the contractual rights it conferred on the wife and son subject to the Act, and the statutory rights it provided for the daughter of the deceased?

As noted above, the High Court decided that Deed and contractual rights were subject to the FPA provisions under the Act.

The central issue of the case was to determine what effect the operation of the Act had on the Deed and the annexed mutual wills which were executed pursuant to that Deed.

In particular, it was argued by the wife and the son as the First and Second Respondents that the decision in Schaefer and that of Nicholls CJ in *Re Richardson's Estate* (1935) 29 Tas LR 149 should be followed. It was argued that the rights of a party to a deed do not arise under the will but arise contractually in accordance with the terms of the deed entered into between the parties. Accordingly, it would be inappropriate for such contractual rights to be reduced to what effectively becomes a gift under the will.

Lord Cross in Schaefer followed the reasoning of Nicholls CJ in Richardson and rejected the notion that the performance of the contract by a party to leave their estate to another then turns the other party to the agreement from a creditor into a mere beneficiary.

However, in both Richardson and Schaefer, there was dissenting opinion against the argument that statutory rights could not make inroads to the contractual obligations created or entered into prior to death. Firstly, Clarke J in Richardson argued that the contract in that case was that the testator would make a will and leave his estate to the Respondent in consideration of them agreeing to remain his housekeeper for little or no remuneration until his death. The testator did this and therefore completed his contractual obligations.

Accordingly, the estate was under no liability to the housekeeper, as the deceased had performed his promise and left the estate to the housekeeper in his will. However, this does not mean that the estate cannot then be affected by statute, as the housekeeper's rights must be considered alongside the rights of those who may apply for provision under the Act.

Lord Simon in Schaefer dissented, preferring to follow the decision in Dillon. In Lord Simon's opinion, a promisee's contractual or equitable rights will fail to be considered along with a dependant's statutory rights for provision.

Ultimately then, despite the decision in Barns, the effect of the FPA legislation can always be avoided by disposition of the estate before death so that the deceased dies with no estate. However, the rights a promisee obtains under a deed are always liable to be affected by the potential operation of the Act where the estate has not been so disposed of prior to death.

Binding financial agreements

Following on from Barns, a relevant question is whether binding financial agreements entered into between parties where one party subsequently dies still bind the deceased person's personal representative and their estate such that any FPA which is subsequently filed, can only access those assets to which the deceased is entitled under the agreement?

Section 90H Family Law Act states that:

> 'a financial agreement that is binding on the parties to the agreement continues to operate despite the death of a party to the agreement and operates in favour of and is binding on, the legal personal representative of that party.'

The succession legislation in all jurisdictions has modified the common law rule that personal actions did not survive the death of a party such that now all causes of action subsisting against or vesting in the person shall survive against, or, as the case may be, for the benefit of, the person's estate.

Accordingly, it would ordinarily be the case that a binding financial agreement could frustrate any FPA claim which might be brought, particularly where the agreement transfers a substantial portion of the assets to the surviving spouse.

One of the conflicting things to come out of Barns was an affirmation that an order of the Court pursuant to a FPA has the effect of being a codicil to the will of the deceased executed immediately before death. As such, the agreement entered into prior to death would be binding on the estate, preserving certain assets from the FPA applicant, as the FPA order can only draw from the assets of the estate.

In effect, any successful FPA applicant can only be treated as a beneficiary who does not take priority over an estate's creditors or parties with a contractual interest. So is there a difference between the deed of mutual wills which was set aside in Barns and a binding financial agreement? Most commentary suggests there is.

Policy reasons aside, the difference in Barns was that the FPA was brought on the death of the first party to a deed of mutual wills such that the Court was able to determine that the second party to the deed had not yet relied on the deed and had received no valuable consideration. It is likely that the Court would have reached an entirely different view if the FPA had been brought against the estate of the surviving party to the deed in Barns when they had died, because they would have relied on the deed and not changed their will or transferred assets or done something else to try and give effect to their wishes.

Accordingly, *Barns* can be said to be limited to the specific circumstances where the first spouse has died after executing mutual wills and does not alter the law in so far as it relates to the effect of mutual wills following the death of the second spouse.

The case also does not change the position that existing contractual obligations bind the estate. Thus, provided there has been consideration given and the parties have relied on the binding financial agreement in some way, then the FPA will not have access to the assets which are subject to the binding financial agreement.

This said however, a binding financial agreement entered into for the sole purpose of defeating a FPA, as opposed to the objects for binding financial agreements as expressed in the *Family Law Act*, may fail for policy reasons to prevent the FPA having access to the assets which are the subject of the binding financial agreement (as occurred in Barns).

The Courts have looked at the relationship between a binding financial agreement (of sorts) and a FPA in the past and most notably in *Smith v Smith* (1986) FLC 91–604 and *Singer v Berghouse* (1994) 181 CLR at 201 where the High Court confirmed that while a clause in a binding financial agreement which bars any claim against the estate of a party (i.e. effectively a double dip) is not binding of itself such a clause (and indeed the binding financial agreement itself), will be given serious consideration by a Court in any proceedings brought for a FPA by a party who has received benefit under the binding financial agreement. What these cases do not say though is whether or not another applicant (that is, someone not a party to the binding financial agreement) could access assets subject to the binding financial agreement for inclusion in their FPA.

Trusts and other asset protection strategies

A Court has the power to make a determination of whether adequate provision has been made for an applicant out of the estate of the deceased person. The rules are similar in each jurisdiction, although there is some difference in wording of the legislation.

In all jurisdictions, the legislation is such that the executor must sell the assets of an estate for realising sufficient funds to meet the debts and legacies of the deceased estate, and in Queensland, an executor is only able to sell the assets of the estate for the purposes of realising sufficient funds to meet the debts of the estate.

Accordingly, any FPA can only be brought against an estate of a person, and as with a beneficiary's rights, will be subject to the debts and encumbrances of the deceased's estate before any payment can be made. This means that transferring assets to a trust or mortgaging assets can be effective strategies for guarding against a FPA. Gleeson CJ in Barns noted that:

> 'First, provision may be made, and can only be made, out of a deceased's estate; that is to say, out of property which is beneficially owned by the deceased at the time of death and which passes to the deceased's legal personal representative.
>
> Secondly, contractual obligations undertaken by a deceased during his lifetime, which bind an estate, may affect the property available to meet an order under the Act. For example, if, during his lifetime, a testator contracted to sell Blackacre, and the contract remained on foot at the time of death, although full beneficial ownership of Blackacre had not passed to the purchaser at the time of death, Blackacre would not be an available asset for the purposes of an order for provision, although the purchase price payable under the contract would be. And, of course, if the contract were subsequently rescinded, the position would change.
>
> Thirdly, the estate out of which an order for provision may be made is the available estate after meeting the liabilities of the deceased. Obligations incurred by a deceased, and binding upon a legal per-

sonal representative, must be taken into account in determining the extent of the estate out of which provision may be made.'

Gleeson CJ went on to say that:

'Reference has already been made to an inherent weakness in the scheme of the Act, and its earlier legislative counterparts, as an instrument to deal with the mischief at which it is aimed. Provision under the Act can only be made out of the assets of which a person dies possessed. If property is not beneficially owned by a deceased, then (subject to later legislative amendments in some jurisdictions) it does not form part of the deceased's estate, and cannot be made a source of provision for a claimant under the Act. Furthermore, contractual obligations undertaken by a person prior to death, which bind the legal personal representative in the administration of the estate, may diminish the available estate out of which provision may be made.'

Gleeson CJ also pointed out that contractual obligations and transactions entered into during a person's life (including, presumably binding death benefit nominations for superannuation savings) would still effectively avoid the FPA provisions, unless the legislation expressly extends to such transactions, as is the case under the *Family Provision Act* 1982 (NSW) and its use of notional estate.

There are of course costs associated with such strategies, including stamp duty and the realisation of potential capital gains.

However, where a will maker is adamant they want protection from a potential FPA, a trust provides an alternative, providing of course that the terms of the deed are appropriately drafted, as the assets which are transferred into the trust will no longer form part of the deceased's estate.

Notional estate

While the use of trusts, mortgages and other strategies may for the time being provide effective protection from a FPA, New South Wales has introduced legislation dealing with 'notional estates' and the ability of a FPA applicant to clawback assets into an estate (i.e. assets transferred during a will maker's life, to a trust for example, to avoid a FPA).

With the national uniform succession laws becoming increasingly likely the use of trusts and similar strategies to prevent a successful FPA being brought will be undermined.

Notional estates allow the Court to look beyond the assets held by the deceased at the date of death and to examine the assets held by the deceased in the years prior to death, when considering a FPA. Effectively it means that contracts entered into whereby the deceased promises their estate to a party, could be subject to an application for provision by a person entitled, such that the promisee effectively becomes a beneficiary and not a debtor of the estate.

The decision in Barns endorses this concept in that it ensures the rights of the promisee do not take priority and are indeed considered alongside the statutory rights granted to an applicant for provision. As noted above however, Barns is limited to the particular circumstances where a testator has promised their estate to a person for valuable consideration or pursuant to a deed.

Child maintenance trusts

Child maintenance trusts are specifically provided for in s 102AGA of the ITAA 1936. As with the estate proceeds trust, super proceeds trust and testamentary trusts, the main advantage of a child maintenance trust is the ability for income of the trust to be treated as excepted trust income.

As discussed above, excepted trust income means that any infant children who are beneficiaries of the trust and are entitled to income of the trust will have access to the normal adult rates of tax (for example the first, approximately, $24,000 worth of income tax-free, with the balance at normal adult rates).

A child maintenance trust, like most trusts, must be established by deed. There are also a number of other requirements that must be met before the income of the trust is treated as excepted, including:

a the children named as the 'primary beneficiaries' of the trust must be younger than 18 at the time the trust is established;
b income must be derived by the investment of property transferred to the trustee of the trust for the benefit of the beneficiary/beneficiaries as a result of a 'family breakdown'. The definition of a 'family breakdown' is relatively wide however reference should always be had on a case by case basis to the definition set out in s 102AGA(1) of the ITAA 1936;
c there is no set time frame in which a child maintenance trust must be established following the family breakdown;
d the children for whom the trust is established to benefit must ultimately receive all of the capital from the trust in equal shares; and
e the potential income beneficiaries of the trust may include persons other than children of the relationship subject to the family breakdown.

The income of a child maintenance trust which results from non arm's length transactions must be of equal value to that which would have been derived on an arm's length basis in order to be considered excepted trust income for the purposes of Div 6AA, for the same reasons discussed above.

One tax effective alternative often used in establishing a child maintenance trust is to contribute depreciating assets such as plant and equipment and motor vehicles to the trust. These assets can be leased either to a related individual or business entity for value.

Provided the lease repayments are on an arm's length basis then the income will be able to be distributed to infant children as excepted trust income.

THE USE OF SPECIAL PURPOSE TRUSTS IN ESTATE PLANNING – PART 2

The use of special purpose trusts in estate planning – part 2

IN LIGHT OF fundamental changes to the taxation regime and the expanding wealth of Australia's aging population, there is a growing need for estate planning to utilise appropriate structuring. This article focuses on the use of special purpose trusts in the estate planning process.

Bankrupt or at risk Beneficiaries

Trusts are often used in an estate planning context to help protect inheritances from attack by the trustee in bankruptcy if it is a concern that the estate may be passed to beneficiaries at risk of bankruptcy. Last year a number of changes to the bankruptcy legislation were introduced and these are discussed below.

Bankruptcy Legislation Amendment (Anti Avoidance) Act 2006

Significant changes were proposed by the *Bankruptcy Legislation Amendment (Anti Avoidance) Bill 2005* ("BLAAAB"), which received assent on 3 May 2006. These changes, now effective in the *Bankruptcy Legislation Amendment (Anti Avoidance) Act 2006* ("BLAAAA") are noted below in respect of the "claw back" rules and will apply to transfers of property made on, or "examinable periods" (see below) which commenced on, or after 28 days following the day of Royal Assent for the Bill – ie from 1 June 2006.

Section 120, 121 and 122 "claw back" rules – including the BLAAAA effect

In considering claims that might be brought by a trustee in bankruptcy, it is relevant to bear in mind the voidable transaction provisions in the *Bankruptcy Act*. These provisions, often referred to as "claw back" provisions, enable the trustee in bankruptcy to trace and reclaim assets that were transferred prior to a person becoming bankrupt. The BLAAAA extends the s 120(3) rule for transfers at less than full value, as noted below.

In particular, a transfer can be overturned, subject to certain exclusions:

a if the transfer took place within two years before the commencement of the bankruptcy where no consideration was paid or where consideration was less than market value (s 120(3)) – the BLAAAA extends this from two years to two years for related entities; or

b if the transfer took place within five years before the commencement of the bankruptcy and at the time of the transfer the person was insolvent, where no consideration was paid or where consideration was less than market value (s 120(1)); or

c if the transfer took place within six months before the commencement of the bankruptcy, the transfer is to a creditor, the creditor obtains a preference, priority or advantage over other creditors and at the time of the transfer the transferor was insolvent (s 122); or

d at any time where the main purpose in making the transfer is to prevent the transferred property from becoming divisible, or to hinder or to delay the process of making property available for division, among creditors (s 121(1)). While the legislation also makes it clear that there are no limits to the way in which the main purpose can be established, it specifically provides that the purpose can be inferred from all the circumstances that at the time of the transfer the transferor was, or was about to become insolvent (s 121(2)). An exclusion in s 121(4) requires the transferee to pay market value; not to have knowledge of the main purpose (the BLAAAA inserts a further test of requiring that they could not reasonably have inferred); and could not have inferred the actual or imminent insolvent status of the bankrupt transferor.

e It should be remembered that, as the commencement of the bankruptcy may be dated from the first act of bankruptcy within the six months before a relevant petition was presented, up to a further six months could be added to these periods of "claw back".

It is significant to note that, if ss 120 and 121 void ("claw back") the transfer of property, there is a requirement to pay to the transferee the consideration (if any) that they paid.

High Court decision in Cummins – section 121

Importantly, no time limit applies to the class of voidable transactions under s 121.

The provision specifically requires that the main purpose in making the transfer must be to prevent the transferred property from becoming divisible, or to hinder or to delay the process of making property available for division, among creditors.

On 7 March 2006, the High Court handed down its decision in the appeal case *The Trustees of the Property of John Daniel Cummins, A Bankrupt v Cummins* [2006] HCA 6 ("Cummins"), dealing with s 121.

Mr Cummins was a barrister who had not lodged tax returns for a very long time (in fact since 1955 when he was an articled clerk) and, when he was eventually identified by the ATO and lodged returns for the 1992-99 years, was then assessed by the ATO for large amounts – and became bankrupt.

The case related to:

a the transfer (for less than market value) to Mrs Cummins (since divorced from Mr Cummins) of Mr Cummins's 50 percent share in the family home at Hunters Hill in August 1987; and
b the transfer (for less than market value) to a family trust of 6,000 shares in the company which entitled Mr Cummins to occupy his chambers in Sydney City also in August 1987.
c There was a further issue relating to the proportion of ownership of the home (hence whether Mrs Cummins already owned a larger part, which could not then be "clawed back") which is not directly relevant for purposes of this paper.

The High Court decision upheld the original Federal Court decision of Sackville J and overruled the Full Federal Court. The Full Federal Court decision had been largely based on a view that there had been a lack of evidence of the tax liability at the time of the transfers, but the High Court appears to have had little difficulty in rejecting this approach.

The High Court comments in relation to the practical application of s 121 are of critical importance.

For s 121 to apply, there must (at the time of the subject transfer of property) be:

a the probability that the property would have been available to creditors if it had not been transferred (s 121(1)(a)); and
b the relevant main purpose of preventing the transferred property from becoming divisible, or to hinder or to delay the process of making property so available (s 121(1)(b)).

The High Court concluded that Sackville J did not err when he concluded that there was a tax liability which made the ATO a creditor at the time of the transfers. Interestingly though, in the Court's view these 1987 and earlier liabilities were not the 1992-99 year liabilities, which were actually later assessed and claimed by the ATO.

Unfortunately, this conclusion meant that the Court did not need to consider the question that would be more relevant to most of us (but which is mentioned at para 31 of the judgment)–whether plaintiffs under potential actions for professional negligence could also be taken to be **creditors** for the purposes of s 121.

This is a critical point. Generally, it has been thought that if there is no existing claim then there is no creditor–but Mr Cummins had a tax liability even though the formal assessment processes to raise a debt had not occurred.

Instead, the lack of any knowledge about an actual or likely claim would seem instead to be taken into account in relation to the main purpose. Thus, if an individual does not (on a reasonable basis) have any reason to believe that a claim could be made and has no existing issue with meeting payments to (known) creditors, then it would be difficult to demonstrate that a transfer can have been made for either of the purposes in s 121(1)(b).

From *Cummins* it can be noted that in being satisfied that Mr Cummins had one of the required main purposes:

a Sackville J originally concluded that Mr Cummins was "well aware in August 1987" of substantial tax liabilities and that the ATO would assess those liabilities as soon as the ATO became aware, which could be at any time;

b the High Court rejected alternative explanations of the August 1987 transactions;

c that they were to benefit the family–as minor and in any case consistent with defeating or delaying creditors;

d as being within the terms of the decision in Williams v Lloyd (1934) 50 CLR 341–on the basis that in that case the husband transferor was 'in a perfectly sound financial position' with 'nothing to fear'; and

e as being to protect against future creditors–on the basis of the High Court agreeing with Sackville J in his earlier decision, that the transfers were instead directed at defeating or delaying the ATO.

The reference to *Williams V Lloyd* raises some hope that a sound existing financial position, without any known or expected claims, would prevent s 121 from applying, but again the High Court did not feel it necessary to fully explore the 'future creditor' issue–and so *Cummins* cannot provide us with definitive comfort on this point. In the leading judgment from *Williams v Lloyd Dixon J* stressed that the real intent to defeat or delay creditors must in fact exist from all the circumstances of a transaction.

BLAAAA–Division 4A changes

Very significant changes were introduced by the BLAAAA for the separate 'clawback' rules under Div 4A of Part VI of the *Bankruptcy Act* for interests in property which have been acquired or which have increased in value due to the bankrupt's (earlier) financial contributions, where the bankrupt has also derived some (direct or indirect) benefit from the property.

These changes essentially expand Div 4A to include natural persons (thereby including spouses, where previously they were excluded and Div 4A was largely ineffective) and also expand the concept of the "examinable period" (during which the relevant "claw back" can occur) as being:

a from four years, or from an earlier first instance of insolvency, up to five years (one more year), from the commencement of the bankruptcy – where a related party has the property interest; and

b from two years, or from an earlier first instance of insolvency, up to five years (three more years), from the commencement of the bankruptcy – where an unrelated party has the property interest.

The most important specific provisions inserted are stated in full below:

'139DA Order relating to property of natural person
If, on an application under s 139A for an order in relation to a respondent entity that is a natural person, the Court is satisfied that:

a during the examinable period, the entity acquired an estate in particular property as a direct or indirect result of financial contributions made by the bankrupt during that period; and
b the bankrupt used, or derived (whether directly or indirectly) a benefit from, the property at a time or times during the examinable period;
c the entity still has the estate in the property;

the Court may make an order of a kind referred to in subs 139D(2) and (3), whether or not the bankrupt has ever had an estate in the property.

139EA Order relating to increase in value of property of natural person
If, on an application under s 139A for an order in relation to a respondent entity that is a natural person, the Court is satisfied that:

a during the examinable period, the value of the entity's interest in particular property increased as a direct or indirect result of financial contributions made by the bankrupt during that period; and
b the bankrupt used, or derived (whether directly or indirectly) a benefit from, the property at a time or times during the examinable period;

the Court may, by order, direct the entity to pay to the applicant a specified amount not exceeding the amount by which the value of the entity's interest in the property increased as a result of the financial contributions made by the bankrupt.'

Some of the immediate questions that arise from these amendments are:

a what will be included as "financial contributions"? – for example, the payment of other bills so that one spouse can pay the mortgage;

b is the value of an interest in property to be taken to increase due to a related liability being paid off? – where the "interest" itself (say 100 percent ownership) will not have not changed; and

c will market value increases be included as being indirectly linked to financial contributions paying off the cost of acquisition?

d Orders (under ss 139D(2) and (3)) may be made to either transfer of all or part of the subject property pursuant to s 139DA, or payment of a specified amount relating to the increased interest in the property pursuant to s 139EA.

These provisions represent a serious threat to the whole strategy of accumulating assets in the hands of "low risk" entities, where value must be "moved" (a financial contribution) to that "low risk" entity – such as is always the case where a professional practices as an individual and (for income in excess of supportable service trust distributions) the practitioner must then gift value to their spouse or other "low risk" entity over time. The ATO push on service trust arrangements obviously exacerbates this problem for many professionals.

The only effective solution to "claw back" provisions of this scope is to structure so that the income from the practice (or other business) is directly earned (and therefore derived for tax purposes) by a "low risk" entity (ie someone or an entity other than the professional).

BLAAAA – other

Finally, it is important to note a number of other changes made by BLAAAA, largely as summarised in the Explanatory Memorandum include the following:

a introduction of a rebuttable presumption of insolvency for the purposes of the "claw back" provisions where a bankrupt has failed to keep proper books, accounts and records;

b voiding (under s 120) a transfer made to defeat creditors if it was reasonable for the transferee to infer that the bankrupt's main purpose in transferring the property was to defeat creditors;

c allowing transcripts and notes from examinations under ss 77C and 81 of the Act to be used in proceedings under the Act, regardless of whether the person examined is a party to the proceedings;

d ensuring that, where the consideration for an earlier property transfer by a bankrupt is paid by a transferee directly to a third party, the property constituting that consideration is itself treated for s 120 and 121 purposes as a (further) transfer by the bankrupt;

e clarification of s 120 to make it clear that a transfer will only be protected from this provision if market value consideration is given by the transferee to the bankrupt; and

f amendments to ss 120 and 121 to make it clear that:

  (i) the amount to be refunded to the transferee by the trustee is the amount that the transferee gave to the bankrupt; and

  (ii) "consideration" for the purposes of these provisions is not to include any right that the transferee has given to their bankrupt spouse to reside at the transferred property (except in the case of marital breakdown).

Division 6AA issues and tax

It is generally accepted that TDTs do provide scope for tax planning opportunities, provided the arrangements entered into are capable of being characterised as arm's length dealings (albeit that the parties involved may not necessarily be at arm's length). For example, income from an arrangement involving a TDT increasing its income earning ability by borrowing on an arm's length basis would still fall within

Div 6AA of the ITAA 1936, whereas, income from gifts or distributions from other "related" individuals or entities will not.

The specific issues that are often raised in the context of the tax planning opportunities under Div 6AA are as follows:

a is excepted trust income limited only to that income which derives from property held by the deceased at the date of their death? In other words, do the underlying capital assets always have to remain the same or can these assets be disposed of and new assets acquired within the trust structure and would income from new assets enjoy the excepted status?
b assuming that the underlying capital assets can be changed, what, if any, limitations are placed on the types of changes that can take place, and in particular can the total capital value of the trust be increased, by way of:
   (i) a TDT going to a bank and borrowing money and then utilising this money in addition to its existing capital to purchase new assets? If so, can all of the income from the asset acquired both with existing TDT money and a loan from a bank enjoy excepted trust income status or does some sort of apportionment need to take place?;
   (ii) distributions made from other trusts to a TDT thereby increasing the capital available for investment via a TDT with all income from this new investment enjoying the excepted trust income rates?; and
   (iii) a beneficiary of a TDT gifting money to a TDT?
c Finally, if income is originally sourced from a TDT but is then distributed via a trust established prior to death to an infant beneficiary, does it retain its status as excepted trust income?

Each of these issues will be dealt with in turn. In all of these situations it is of course necessary to consider the specific anti-avoidance provisions set out in Div 6AA, and the general anti-avoidance provisions set out in Part IVA; however these provisions are outside the scope of this paper.

Is Division 6AA limited to income derived from estate assets?

No. Subsections 102AG(2)(a)(i) and 102AG(2)(d)(i) are the relevant provisions.

Under (a)(i) excepted trust income is the amount which is assessable income of a trust estate that resulted from a will, codicil or court order varying a will or codicil. Importantly, the subsection only prescribes how the trust estate is deemed to have arisen and does not place any limitations on the management of the trust estate, or on the assets which the trust may hold.

The fact that estate assets forming part of the trust estate may be realised and others may be acquired has no implications on the validity of a TDT, nor the ability of the trustee of a TDT to treat the income as excepted. Similarly, if the trustee decides to borrow money and acquire assets which earn income, then Div 6AA applies to that income.

What limitations might be imposed

Section 102AG(3) contains an exception for non-arm's length arrangements. In particular, it provides that if any two or more parties to:

a. the derivation of the excepted trust income mentioned in subs (2); or
b. any act or transaction directly or indirectly connected with the derivation of that excepted trust income;
c. were not dealing with each other at arm's length in relation to the derivation of income, or in relation to the act or transaction, the excepted trust income is only so much (if any) of that income as would have been derived if they had been dealing with each other at arm's length in relation to the derivation, or in relation to the act or transaction.

Essentially this means that if, say, the loan was not at arm's length, but at a more favourable interest rate compared with the market, then the income derived would have been less, and therefore the amount which can be treated as excepted trust income is reduced.

The case of *The Trustee for the Estate of the late AW Furse No. 5 Will Trust v FCT* 91 ATC 4007 is one of the few reported decisions dealing with Div 6AA. In that case Hill J said it was only necessary that the parties be dealing on an arm's length basis and that it was not necessary that they be arm's length parties. Consequently, a loan by a non-arm's length party of itself will not invoke s 102AG(3) unless the parties are also not dealing at arm's length in relation to the terms of the loan.

Income from distributions by trusts established prior to death will not enjoy excepted trust income status because the parties are not dealing at arm's length, unless the trustee gives arm's length consideration for the payment. In the Furse case it was held that where a TDT had acquired a unit in a unit trust, some time after the establishment of the TDT, the income received via distributions from the unit trust was excepted trust income as the acquisition of the unit was on arm's length terms.

TDT distributions to infant beneficiary via inter vivos trust

Where there is a distribution of income from a TDT to an *inter vivos trust*, and then to an infant beneficiary, the better view appears to be that the distribution does not have the status of excepted trust income.

Section 102AG(1) requires that a trust have a prescribed person (essentially an infant, subject to certain exceptions in s 102AC(2)) as a beneficiary. Although it could be argued that a TDT has, as its ultimate beneficiary, an infant, and although s 102AG(1) does not expressly exclude an indirect interest as a beneficiary, s 102AG(1) is likely to be construed as dealing only with direct beneficiaries of a TDT.

Having said this, there is an argument that the income of the "trust estate" contemplated in the opening words to s 102AG(2) need not be the same trust estate, and that the income received by an infant beneficiary via an existing family trust is excepted trust income "in relation to a beneficiary of the trust estate (that is the family trust) to the extent to which the amount–is assessable income of a trust estate (that is the TDT) that resulted from – (i) a will".

Superannuation and Death Benefits

The provision of death benefits is a central object of virtually every superannuation fund. The sole purpose test mentions it amongst both the core and ancillary purposes for which a superannuation fund may be maintained, and it is rare for any superannuation fund not to provide for death benefits. Indeed, certain superannuation funds are established solely to provide death benefits, with the only significant asset of such funds being a life insurance policy.

A significant amount of wealth is now held within the superannuation environment. For many, superannuation benefits will represent the largest or second largest asset behind their family home. Those focused on building wealth through superannuation often prefer to do so through a Self Managed Superannuation Fund ("SMSF"), either to avail themselves of the ability to acquire business real property from themselves and hold such property within the fund, or simply to have more direct control over the fund through trusteeship of the fund.

A natural extension of that desire to control one's wealth is the ability of an individual to put in place an estate plan to deal with their inevitable death. It is somewhat ironic, however, that there have been recent attacks by the government on the use of superannuation in the context of estate planning. The review of the provision of pensions in small superannuation funds notes that "the Government regards the use of superannuation specifically for estate planning rather than retirement income purposes as inconsistent with the purpose of providing tax concessions to superannuation". As a consequence of that report, the government introduced measures to limit the ability of SMSFs and other small superannuation funds to provide defined benefit pensions.

Whilst there is some merit in the view that tax concessions should only be available with respect to the funding required for one's retirement, such an approach can lead to anomalous results. It discourages savings – something which the government otherwise wants to promote. It also suggests that people should avoid being frugal in their retirement, lest they die leaving a substantial unpaid superannuation benefit.

At a time when people are living longer, and the government is seeking to have less people rely on public welfare, discouraging the build up of superannuation entitlements seems to be contradictory. Further, the view of the government appears to assume that people are able to predict with certainty the timing of their death, or at least be able to avoid a "premature" death.

Appointment of trustees after death of a member

The general rules regarding the trusteeship of SMSFs are modified in the event of a member's death. A superannuation fund does not fail to satisfy the relevant tests by reason only that a member of the fund has died and the legal personal representative of the member is a trustee of the fund or a director of a body corporate that is the trustee of the fund, in the place of the member, during the period beginning when the member died and ending when death benefits commence to be payable in respect of the member of the fund.

Although these provisions might be seen as merely a practical consequence given the general requirements of the legislation, there are important implications that can flow. The selection of executors by a member of a SMSF can have impacts outside that member's estate, where the executors become trustees (or directors of the corporate trustee) of the SMSF of which the testator was a member. The trustees will often have a discretion regarding the payment of a death benefit, and often an executor will also be a person in whose favour that discretion might be exercised.

For example, a testator with two children might appoint only one of those children as his executor. Notwithstanding that the will may be quite specific about the division of the testator's estate, the executor may retain a discretion regarding the distribution of the testator's superannuation death benefit. The executor might, in that case, determine to pay the whole of the death benefit to himself or herself to the exclusion of the sibling.

Moreover, it is relevant to note that the appointment of the executor in the member's place as a trustee or trustee director is not automatic. This is highlighted in the recent decision of Katz v Grossman [2005] NSWSC 934.

This case involved a dispute between a sister and brother regarding their father's death benefit. The father had established a superannuation fund in 1965, which became a SMSF. In May 1983 the father appointed his wife as an additional trustee of the fund. She passed away in 1998.

On 18 May 1999 the father appointed his daughter as an additional trustee of the fund. In August 2003 the daughter became a member of the fund. In September 2003 the father passed away. Three months later in December 2003 the daughter appointed her husband as an additional trustee of the fund.

The brother launched legal action against his sister and her husband, claiming that their appointments were invalid. The brother claimed that his sister's appointment was not ratified by a majority of members as required by the trust deed and this meant the father had no capacity to appoint his daughter. This in turn meant that her husband's appointment was invalid because she did not have valid trustee powers.

The sister argued that the appointment was valid because there was no majority of members able and willing to act at the time of her appointment, except for her father. She claimed that her father was entitled to appoint her.

She raised an alternative argument that her father had the power of two votes, being his own and a second vote as executor of his wife's estate under s 44 of the *Wills Probate and Administration Act* 1898 (NSW).

It was held that the sister's appointment was valid. The fact that there was no appointment 19 months after the death of the mother meant that no authorised person acted within the reasonable time. This situation, therefore, satisfied the requirements of the Trustee Act 1925 (NSW) and the father was entitled to appoint his daughter as an additional trustee.

On the second issue of her husband's appointment, the court also ruled in favour of the sister, holding that the Trustee Act also applied to the appointment of her husband.

This meant that her decision to appoint her husband was valid at law. The fact that both the brother and sister were executors, and therefore entitled to be appointed as trustees of the fund was not relevant as there was in fact no such appointment (nor any requirement to make such appointment).

Ultimately, the sister's position as one of the existing trustees enabled her to take control of the fund, irrespective of her father's wishes.

Payment of death benefits

As announced in the 2006 Federal Budget, the superannuation legislative provisions relating to the payment of death benefits are currently under review and the following discussion is deliberately limited to the way in which the superannuation provisions apply and not the tax related issues.

As superannuation is held in trust the payment of proceeds upon death is generally not governed by the terms of the deceased's will. It is normally up to the trustee of the relevant fund to determine whether a person's superannuation benefits are paid to a dependant directly or to their estate. A superannuation fund trustee can only pay a superannuation death benefit to a dependant or to a deceased's legal personal representative.

Under superannuation laws a dependant is:

a a person's spouse (including a de facto spouse at the time of death and a former spouse);

b a person's child (including a stepchild, ex-nuptial or adopted child);
c a person who is financially dependent on the deceased at the time of death.
d There are two types of nominations that the trustee may provide, being:
e a non-binding nomination; and
f a binding nomination.
g When a person makes a non-binding nomination they are informing the trustee of the fund the persons to whom they wish their superannuation benefits to be paid.

The trustee is not legally bound to comply with a non-binding death benefit nomination, although the trustee is legally required to take it into account in deciding to whom the superannuation benefits are to be paid to upon death.

If the fund allows it, a member may make a binding nomination. A binding nomination is a written election made by the member that directs the trustee of the fund to pay the benefit to any dependants or to their executor.

The trustee is legally bound to comply with the binding nomination so effectively the trustee's discretion has been removed.

Other than where absolute certainty is required as to where any benefits remaining in a fund will be paid on death, it is normally preferable that complete discretion is left with the trustee of the fund as to where and how the remaining benefits in the fund will be paid.

The main reason for recommending this approach is that the taxation and related laws dealing with the payments of the benefits from superannuation funds, as well as the circumstances of the potential beneficiaries of an estate, will continue to change. Rather than trying to predict what the best outcome will be today, it is normally better to leave this decision until it actually needs to be made.

There will however be situations where a binding death benefit nomination is appropriate. For example, there may be concerns that the estate of the member will be the subject of a FPA. In this situation it may be appropriate for the member to put in place a binding nomination in favour of, say, a dependant directly, rather than to have the benefit potentially flow to the estate and be the subject of the claim.

It is relevant to note that the regulations appear to provide that a nomination lapses three years after it was last signed, confirmed or amended. There is a view, however, that this requirement does not apply to SMSFs, and that non-lapsing binding death benefit nominations can be implemented. This approach argues that the general prohibition in s 59(1) of *Superannuation (Industry) Supervision Act 1993* against someone other than the trustee exercising a discretion, expressly does not apply to SMSFs, and that consequently the carve-out in s 59(1A) and the provisions in regulation 6.17A regarding binding death benefit nominations do not apply to SMSFs.

Acknowledgement

Thank you for the contribution of the co-authors of the original articles. Special thanks also to Ash Chotai of Chotais Chartered Accountants for undertaking the peer review.

Matthew Burgess, Partner

TRUST ASSETS AND ESTATE PLANNING: HOW HAS THE DUST SETTLED AFTER KENNON V SPRY?

Trust assets and estate planning: how has the dust settled after *Kennon v Spry*?

Abstract:

IN RECENT YEARS, there have been numerous developments which have challenged the effectiveness of trust structures, causing a loss of faith in the ability of traditional family discretionary trusts to protect assets in the event of marriage breakdown. The High Court decision in Kennon v Spry, in particular, appears to alter longstanding principles relating to the asset protection advantages of trusts in this context. This article considers the consequences of that decision, discusses the treatment of trust assets in a relationship breakdown and the distinction between assets forming part of the pool of property or being treated as a financial resource, examines the application of these principles in recent decisions, and offers some practical recommendations. The authors conclude that, while this is an evolving area of law, recent case law indicates that, for the foreseeable future, well-structured trusts should continue to be an effective vehicle for asset protection and estate planning.

Introduction

Recent years have been a turbulent time for the controllers of trusts and their advisers.

Some of the developments challenging the effectiveness of trust structures that have taken place have included:

(1) amendments to the bankruptcy legislation to widen the situations in which trust assets might be exposed in the event of an individual associated with the trust becoming bankrupt;

(2) continuing attempts (which to date have been unsuccessful) by trustees in bankruptcy to argue that the power of appointment over trust assets is of itself an asset of a bankrupt person capable of being exercised by the trustee in bankruptcy;

(3) numerous changes to the application of the Div 7A tax regime to capture and tax arrangements where unpaid present entitlements have arisen following a distribution from a discretionary trust;

(4) the *Richstar*[1] decision, which called into question the level of asset protection that a discretionary trust can provide if a controller of a trust personally becomes bankrupt. The Richstar decision arguably took on further significance when the presiding judge, Justice French, subsequently became Chief Justice of the High Court;

(5) the government's decision to abolish the capital gains tax exemption for trust cloning in late 2008, which stripped the owners of many family trusts of the ability to restructure their trusts to achieve asset protection or succession planning objectives; and

(6) the decisions in *Bamford*,[2] *Colonial*[3] and *Clark*[4] and subsequent Taxation Office and government responses.

While all of the above issues have required (in some instances significant) additional planning, for a combination of reasons, family discretionary trusts are still often viewed as the structure of choice for many business owners and private investors. In recent times, however, many advisers and clients alike have, perhaps unnecessarily, lost faith in the ability of trusts to protect assets in the event of a marriage[5] breakdown.

Arguably, the most significant cause of this lack of confidence in trusts is the High Court decision of Kennon v Spry6, on the basis that it appears to alter the longstanding principles relating to the asset protection advantages of trusts in the context of a marriage breakdown.

This article considers:

(1) the consequences of the decision in *Kennon v Spry*;
(2) discussion about the treatment of trust assets in a relationship breakdown and the distinction between assets forming part of the pool of property or being treated as a financial resource;
(3) the application of these principles in recent decisions;
(4) some practical recommendations when dealing with trusts in the context of estate planning and structuring clients' affairs; and
(5) whether a trust can still be an effective tool to protect assets from exposure to relationship breakdowns.

For completeness, references to trusts in this article mean traditional family discretionary trusts. Some time will be devoted to exploring the impact of various trust structuring nuances.

Summary of the core principles: the Family Courts' powers to deal with trust assets

Asset protection principles relating to trusts

THE ASSET PROTECTION typically understood to be afforded by trusts is derived from the longstanding view that a mere discretionary beneficiary of a trust does not have a proprietary interest in a trust's assets, and the main right of a discretionary beneficiary is limited to enforcing due administration by the trustee. Consequently, it is difficult to value this right when the beneficiary has no present entitlement to the trust's assets and may never have any entitlement to any part of the income or capital of the discretionary trust.

While this has been the accepted view for hundreds of years, recent decisions in Australia potentially undermine the level of asset protection afforded by trusts.

The high-profile decision of *Richstar* considered whether a beneficiary can have a proprietary interest in the assets of a trust where that beneficiary has 'effective control' over the trust.

In *Richstar*, the court held that some of the defendants had 'at least a contingent interest' in the trust property, which was sufficient for the property to be potentially available to the receivers. A contingent interest was found to arise where 'the trustee is effectively the alter ego of the relevant beneficiary or otherwise subject to his or its effective control'.

Although the court did not allow the full order sought by ASIC, the decision challenged the traditional view that a beneficiary of a discretionary trust has no more than a mere 'expectancy' that of itself is not sufficient to constitute 'property' which is available to creditors.

For completeness, it should be noted that *Richstar* was a decision about proprietary interests in a bankruptcy context. As the focus of this article is on the proprietary interest of a beneficiary of a trust in the context of the Family Law Courts, the *Richstar* decision is not discussed any further.

Similarly, although included in the title of this article, the facts of *Kennon v Spry* are not set out in full. For those interested in understanding in more detail the circumstances surrounding *Kennon v Spry*, the excellent papers written by Arlene Macdonald for the Tax Institute's 2010 Tax Intensive[7] and Ken Schurgott for the Tax Institute's 2011 Tax Intensive[8] are highly recommended.

Kennon v Spry

In 1968, the husband settled a discretionary trust named the ICF Spry Trust, of which he was both the trustee and settlor. The eligible beneficiaries consisted of the 'standard' range of beneficiaries typically found in a discretionary trust, including the husband, any spouse of the husband, the husband's issue, his siblings, their spouses and their issue, and charitable beneficiaries.

In 1978, the husband and the wife married and they subsequently had four daughters.

In 1983, the husband varied the trust deed by excluding himself as a beneficiary and appointing the wife as trustee on his death or resignation. As a result, the husband ceased to be a potential beneficiary. It was understood that this variation was done predominantly for land tax purposes.

In December 1998, at a time when the wife argued that the relationship was starting to strain, the husband executed a further deed of variation which excluded the wife as a capital beneficiary.

During the course of 2002, the husband established a discretionary trust for each of the four daughters of the marriage, of which he was the initial trustee and was later the joint trustee with a Mr Edwin Philip Kennon. As trustee of the ICF Spry Trust, the husband then distributed the capital and income of that trust equally between the four children's trusts.

Following the couple's separation and subsequent divorce, the wife sought orders from the court setting aside the distributions from the ICF Spry Trust to the children's trusts, arguing that the pool of assets for distribution should include the ICF Spry Trust's assets and the income distributed to the children's trusts.

The primary question before the court was whether the pool of assets for distribution on the property settlement should comprise the assets of the ICF Spry Trust. The wife argued that the pool should include the assets in the children's trusts, while the husband alleged that neither the ICF Spry Trust, nor any of the children's trusts, could be considered property or indeed even a financial resource of the parties to the marriage.

The trial judge made orders to set aside the 1998 and 2002 instruments and ordered that the assets of the ICF Spry Trust be included in the pool of assets for division between the parties.

On appeal (ultimately) to the High Court, the majority held (among other things) that the husband's legal ownership of the assets as sole trustee, combined with the wife's interest as a beneficiary of the trust, were a proper basis for the assets of the ICF Spry Trust to be treated as the property of the parties.

What Kennon v Spry means for trusts

Initially, Kennon v Spry raised concerns that the decision represented a significant widening of the courts' power to effectively disregard the existence of a trust when considering the division of assets on a property settlement.

Over time, the practical impact of the decision has arguably softened, not least of which due to the fact that the outcome of the decision appears to be strongly linked to the somewhat unique circumstances of the case. In particular, the arguably questionable conduct by the husband (such as mismanagement of trust assets, threatened destruction of trust assets, misleading representations to the courts, and attempted direct communication with the judges) may have contributed significantly to the outcome.

A number of cases since 2008 reinforce the conclusion that the impact of Kennon v Spry has not been as severe as initially feared. However, before exploring some of the cases in this regard, it is relevant to consider the underlying powers conferred on the courts in relation to trusts by the Family Law Act 1975 (Cth).

Powers in the Family Law Act relating to trusts

THE SUMMARY BELOW is intended to give only a 'high-level' introduction to the powers of the Family Court, to provide context when considering the decisions following *Kennon v Spry*. For a comprehensive summary of the court's powers relating to trusts, Arlene Macdonald's paper mentioned above is again suggested as recommended reading.

The meaning of 'property' in the Family Law Act

The starting point of a property division is determining the nature of the assets and liabilities of the parties to the marriage, and to classify those assets and liabilities as either property of the parties or a financial resource or, potentially, neither. If a court determines as part of this process that a trust's assets fall under the definition of a financial resource (as opposed to being the property of the parties), then those assets cannot be divided between the parties under a court order.

Table 1 provides a diagrammatic summary of the options available to the court when dealing with assets of the marriage.

Table 1

Not property or a financial resource	Is a financial resource	Is property but only a portion represents property of the marriage	Is property and 100% should be treated as property of the marriage

The Family Law Act defines 'property' as 'property to which those parties are, or that party is, as the case may be, entitled, whether in possession or reversion'.[9] If an asset is property of a party to a marriage, the Family Law Act confers a wide power on the court to vary the legal interests in the property and to make orders for a settlement of property in substitution for any interest in the property.[10]

The definition of property in the Family Law Act can be contrasted with the definition under the *Bankruptcy Act* 1966 (Cth), which states that property is 'real or personal property of every description ... and includes any estate, interest or profit, whether present or future, vested or contingent, arising out of or incident to any such real or personal property'.[11]

Due to the very broad definition of property in the Family Law Act, the Family Court therefore has a much wider ability to deal with trust property than the courts dealing with other regimes, for example, bankruptcy.

Thus, in *Kennon v Spry*, the court held that where:

(1) the husband was (at the relevant junctures) the sole trustee and appointor; and
(2) the trustee had absolute discretion to vary the terms of the trust deed and distribute income and capital to any one or more of the beneficiaries to the exclusion of any,

this was indicative that the husband was the sole controller of the trust.

The husband's control role (which meant that the husband had the discretionary power to transfer all assets of the trust to the wife), together with the wife's right of due administration as a beneficiary of the trust, was sufficient justification for the court to determine that the assets of the ICF Spry Trust should be treated as property of the parties.

One developing issue in this regard (which is outside the scope of this article but warrants mention) relates to the so-called 'Jodee Rich'[12] amendments that, in certain situations, empower the Family

Court to make decisions that simultaneously bind the parties to the marriage breakdown and various third parties, including creditors.

This power arose from O'Ryan J's judgment in the matter of *Australian Securities and Investments Commission & Rich:*[13]

> '... I have no jurisdiction to make the orders sought by ASIC pursuant to s 90K ... However, it is of concern to me that the consequence of my finding is that the Family Court has no jurisdiction to deal with an application by an unsecured or contingent creditor to set aside a financial agreement in circumstances where the interests of such a third party are or may be adversely affected by the terms of the agreement ... It was therefore entered into to defeat the interests of third parties
>
> ... In my view, consideration should be given to conferring jurisdiction on this Court to deal with an application by the third party whose interests may be adversely affected by the terms of a binding financial agreement to set aside the agreement. There are public policy reasons for why this should be so. Thus Part VIIIA should be reviewed, at least in terms of its effect on the legitimate interests of third parties, because the Family Law Act may be made ... an instrument of harm to a third party.'

Section 79 of the Family Law Act 1975

SECTION 79 OF the *Family Law Act 1975* applies where the court finds that the trust assets are property of a party to the marriage, rather than a financial resource. Broadly, the four powers of the court in relation to assets held via a trust are as follows:

(1) bringing assets notionally into the matrimonial property pool;
(2) setting aside transactions which would have the effect of diminishing claims under the Family Law Act;
(3) declaring the purported trust arrangements to be a sham; and
(4) altering the ownership of a third party and making binding orders on third parties.[14]

Determining the 'notional' pool of assets

As set out above, arguably the most important step in the making of a property settlement by the court is the process of determining the 'pool' of assets available for distribution. Where there is clear evidence that one spouse is the true, unilateral controller of a trust holding assets accrued throughout the marriage of the parties, as well as a potential beneficiary, the court will treat the trust assets as the property of the parties. In these situations, the assets of the trust will be automatically added to the pool.

In *Beeson & Spence*,[15] it was held that, where trust assets are in fact used for the benefit of one (or both) of the parties of the marriage, the court can 'look through' the formal legal ownership by the trustee when determining the pool of assets.

The rationale for these powers is that it would be contrary to public policy to allow a spouse with full control of assets to quarantine them via a trust from property settlement proceedings where the controlling spouse has the power to determine at any point to whom income and/or capital will be distributed, including to themselves.

Setting aside transactions

The court has power under s 106B of the *Family Law Act 1975* to set aside attempts to alter a trust relationship for the purpose of preventing the court from adding the assets of the trust to the property pool.

In *Kennon v Spry*, the court relied on this power to set aside the 1998 and 2002 instruments on the basis that the amendments were undertaken for the purpose of limiting the wife's access to the assets of the trust in any subsequent property settlement. At face value, the use of the power in s 106B by the court appeared to create a situation where the assets of a trust could be fully exposed, even where:

(1) neither party to the marriage solely controlled the trusteeship of a trust; or
(2) neither party to the marriage were beneficiaries of the trust.

While the husband in *Kennon v Spry* argued that it should be the four children's trusts (of which he was only a co-trustee, and neither he nor the wife were beneficiaries) that should be the subject of the court proceedings, by relying on s 106B, the court effectively ignored the establishment of those trusts and the purported removal of the wife as a potential beneficiary of the original trust.

Having effectively redefined the structure of the trusts, the decision in Kennon v Spry ultimately became a relatively 'standard' application of how the Family Court determines the notional pool of assets and should be seen as an extension of the powers as previously understood in s 106B.

Sham trusts

The courts also have power to effectively ignore a trust structure where the trust arrangement is, in fact, a sham. A trust will be treated as a sham (and its purported existence ignored) where the parties intended to create rights and obligations different from those described in the documents. Before a document is held to be a sham, it must be shown that there was the intention to mislead third parties in respect of the relevant rights and obligations in dispute.[16]

The relatively recent decision of *Harris & Harris*[17] is an example of the court considering whether a trust arrangement was in fact a sham. In that case, the trust had been established at the instigation of the father of the husband prior to the husband's marriage.

'... the exercise of these powers must be supported by the underlying factual circumstances.'

The trustee of the trust was a company of which the husband and his sister and mother were directors. The husband's mother held 50% of the shares, and the husband and his sister each held 25% of the shares. At the time of the proceedings, the husband's mother was also the appointor of the trust. The husband was listed as a potential beneficiary of the trust, together with his other family members.

The trust owned, among other assets, all of the shares in a company which ran a business initially operated by the husband and wife and after the separation operated only by the husband.

The wife argued that the control arrangements in place were a sham, and that the trading company (of which there was no dispute that the husband was the managing director) was an alter ego of the husband and, on this basis, the husband had sufficient control of the trust itself such that the assets of both the trust and trading company should be regarded as being included in the property pool.

Alternatively, the wife alleged that the husband's mother was 'a puppet' of the husband, and he had indirect control of the trust through her.

The court applied the principles set out by French CJ in *Kennon v Spry* and found that, while the husband was a 'beneficiary of the trust, he did not control the trustee directly or indirectly ...' and there was no basis to notionally include the assets of the trust (including its shares in the trading company) as part of the pool of assets.

In relation to whether the trust arrangements were effectively a sham, the court found that the wife did not advance sufficient evidence to support a finding that the husband's mother was the husband's 'puppet', through which he exercised de facto control of the trustee company and of the trust.

The fact that the trust had been established by the father of the husband, and that virtually every change in the management and direction of the trust could be at least partially referrable to the ongoing estate and succession planning arrangements of the husband's parents, provided strong support to the conclusion that the trust was not a sham.

Altering third party ownership

Under the powers in ss 90AC and 90AE, the court effectively has power to make the following orders:

(1) direct a third party to do a thing in relation to the property of the marriage, or alter the rights, liabilities or property interests of a third party in relation to the marriage;[18]

(2) restrain a person from repossession of property of a party to the marriage or grant an injunction restraining a person from commencing legal proceedings against a party to the marriage;[19] and

(3) direct a third party to do a thing in relation to the property of the marriage or alter the rights, liabilities or property interests of a third party in relation to the marriage.[20]

The practical implications of this power were demonstrated in the enforcement action following *Kennon v Spry in the matter of Stephens & Stephens (Enforcement)*,[21] where it was held that:[22]

'In our view, it follows that an order may be made that enables an entitlement of a party to the marriage who is an object of the trust, or ceased to be an object by reason of divorce, to be satisfied out of the assets of the trust. Put another way, an order may be made that enables a party to the marriage who is in control of the trust to satisfy his or her personal liability to the other party to the marriage who is an object of the trust from the assets of the trust.'

Decisions following Kennon v Spry

THERE HAVE BEEN a number of reported decisions since *Kennon v Spry* which provide context to the exact scope of the court's powers under s 79 of the *Family Law Act 1975*.

While there is little doubt about the potentially wide scope of the court's powers under s 79, the exercise of these powers must be supported by the underlying factual circumstances. Set out below are summaries of a few of the most relevant cases involving trusts, which in each instance explore one or more of the key themes addressed in *Kennon v Spry*.

The cases explored are summarised under the following four headings, namely:

(1) the manner in which a trust is controlled;
(2) the purpose of the trust on establishment (including the range of potential beneficiaries);
(3) the source of trust assets; and
(4) trusts established as part of an estate plan.

Control of trusts

Beeson & Spence involved a trust established by the wife during the marriage. The wife argued that the trust was established with the purpose of benefitting the children of the relationship and should not be treated as property of the marriage.

On establishment of the trust, the wife's father and her solicitor were appointed as trustees and the wife was the appointor. At a time when the husband was going through financial difficulties, the deed was varied to exclude the wife and the husband as potential beneficiaries of the trust, as well as to resign the wife as appointor. A new appointor, being the wife's sister, was nominated in her place.

The husband argued that the trust was established for the benefit of the family and not just the children.

The court ignored the release of direct control by the wife (through her resignation as the appointor) and held that the wife still retained sufficient control of the trust to support a conclusion that the assets should be treated as property of the marriage, citing the following reasons:[23]

> 'The Deed of Variation recognised the resignation of the wife as the appointor and brought about important and fundamental changes to the Trust by appointing a new appointor and by removing the wife and the husband as beneficiaries in their own right as parents of the specified beneficiaries. Until then, the wife could have continued to lawfully control the Trust by ensuring it was administered in a manner of her choosing, including administered for her sole benefit, both as to income and capital. The recitals to the Deed of Variation suggest the wife's resignation as appointor was preceded by a request from the trustees and that, in turn, was made referable to the trustee's concern at possible insolvency and the Trust fund being placed in jeopardy. Yet whatever the thinking behind it or wherever the motivation lay, the plain fact is that nothing, including a request from the trustees, obliged the wife to relinquish control of the Trust by relinquishing the power to appoint the trustees by whose discretion it is administered.

To the contrary, it was within her singular and unquestionable power to remove the trustees and appoint another at any point. So while the recital suggests the relinquishment of the power of appointment was brought about by the trustees, it was obviously and necessarily done with the wife's co-operation and consent which she was at no time obliged to give. Then, having relinquished control and with the new appointor installed, the Deed was altered to remove the 'parents' as beneficiaries in their own right. The steps taken via the Deed of Variation must be seen as having been taken at the wife's direction.'

In contrast, the recent case of *Morton & Morton*[24] saw the court decide that, as the husband was merely a potential beneficiary and did not in fact control the trust, the trust was not his 'alter ego' on the basis that there was not sufficient control over the trust. Therefore, there was nothing to support a finding that the assets of the trust should be held to be the property of the husband.

In summary, the facts of the case were as follows:

(1) the couple were married approximately 10 years and had no children;
(2) at the time of the relationship breakdown, the husband was a beneficiary of a discretionary trust, the Morton Trust;
(3) the beneficiaries of the trust included the husband, the husband's brother, mother, any grandchildren or remote relatives and any company or trust in which the husband and his brother had an interest;
(4) the trustee of the Morton Trust was a trustee company, J Pty Ltd, of which the husband and his brother were equal shareholders and both were directors;
(5) J Pty Ltd, in turn, owned a 'bucket company' on behalf of the trust, known as T Pty Ltd (to which unpaid present entitlements were owed). The husband's brother was the sole director of T Pty Ltd; and
(6) finally, the husband and his brother were the joint appointors of the Morton Trust.

The wife argued that, as the two brothers each had a 50% share of the Morton Trust and T Pty Ltd, a 50% interest should be treated as the husband's property in the property settlement. The wife claimed that the husband, in his capacity as director of J Pty Ltd, had sufficient control of the trust to support this conclusion.[25]

The husband argued that neither he nor his brother had control of J Pty Ltd as neither had a better right than the other in their standings as directors, shareholders or appointors.

The court accepted the husband's arguments and held that the trust assets should not form part of the property pool. It was the case, as accepted by the husband, that the trust's assets were his financial resource.

The decision largely rejected a number of the wife's arguments based on principles set out in *Kennon v Spry*, and highlights the importance of considering the most appropriate approach to take whenever structuring trust arrangements.

The decision in Harris[26] (summarised above) provides further guidance about the relevance of actual control and, in particular, held as follows:[27]

'In the present case and on the basis of the material before us the husband appears to be no more than a beneficiary of a trust. He is not the appointor of the trust nor does he hold any position in the current trustee company.

On the assumption that by the use of the word 'directly', the Chief Justice was referring to the strict legal position, it therefore cannot be said that the husband 'directly' controls the current trustee. Nor could it be said that he 'directly' controlled the previous trustee.

On the assumption that the reference by the Chief Justice to 'indirect' control of a discretionary trust by a beneficiary was a reference to a 'puppet' situation, in the sense that the person with legal control of the trust is a puppet of the beneficiary, that could be the situation in the present case.

In the sense, that is, of the mother (who is the appointor of the trust, and one of the three directors of the trustee company holding two shares in that company with each of the other two directors holding one share each) being the puppet of the husband. This, as was made clear by Counsel's oral submissions to us, has always been the wife's case.

The difficulty, however, for the wife on this appeal is to be able to point to any evidence which would support a finding that the husband's mother is his puppet, and that it is through her, or perhaps otherwise, that he exercises de facto control of the trustee company and of the Trust.'

Purpose of establishing the trust and range of beneficiaries

THE DECISION OF *Essex & Essex*[28] considered the husband's interest in two family trusts, the S Trust and the N Trust. The circumstances of the case were:

(1) in relation to the S trust, the husband was a default beneficiary, and the two children from the marriage were the capital beneficiaries;
(2) the husband was only a general beneficiary in the N Trust, on the basis that he was the brother of the primary beneficiary;
(3) the assets of the two trusts had largely been contributed by the husband's parents for the purpose of providing for the husband's mother's living expenses, and benefiting the husband and his brother and their bloodline;
(4) the husband had not received distributions from either trust; and
(5) the husband's brother was held by the court to be the controller of both trusts.

It was held in the trial court (and endorsed on appeal) that the assets of the N trust could not be considered to be property of the spouse parties, as it was unlikely that the husband would ever receive distributions from the trust and it was established for the primary benefit of the husband's brother's family.

In reaching his decision, the trial judge considered the control of the trusts:[29]

> 'The facts in this matter are distinguishable from the majority of family law proceedings involving discretionary family trusts. Typically when

discretionary trusts are involved in family law proceedings one of the parties is the appointor and, frequently, that party is also a director or major shareholder in the trustee company. In such scenarios, the requisite degree of control may be established relatively easily. This is a significant distinguishing factor from the present case, where there is little evidence that the husband has or will have control of either of the trusts. Such evidence as exists … is not persuasive.'

The trial judge initially held that the assets of the S trust were not a financial resource. However, this conclusion was overturned on appeal. The trust assets were held to be a financial resource of the husband, on the basis that:

(1) the trust deed terms evidenced a clear intention that the husband should benefit from the trust; and
(2) there was evidence that the husband was likely to receive distributions from the trust following finalising of the matter.

The Full Court stated:[30]

'… The S Trust deed evinces a clear intention that the capital of that trust be distributed on vesting, or at such earlier time as the trustee may determine, to the two children of the marriage, the grandchildren of the husband's mother. It also discloses a clear intent that the husband, as one of the three named income beneficiaries, is entitled to be considered to receive distributions of income until the vesting of the trust.'

On appeal, the court confirmed the conclusion of the trial judge that the trust assets could not be property of the marriage, as the husband did not have control of the trusts, nor had he contributed the assets to the trusts.[31]

The primary questions asked of the Family Court in *Keach & Keach*[32] were whether:

(1) being a potential beneficiary of a trust meant its assets should be included in the pool of property; and

(2) the trust was a sham such that the husband was in fact the true owner of the assets of the trust.

The husband's father had established a separate trust for each of his four children. The husband's trust was referred to in the judgment as 'the Junior Trust'. On establishment, the beneficiaries and residuary beneficiaries named in the schedule of the Junior Trust were the husband and his three siblings. The father's trust ('the Senior Trust') was also later appointed as a discretionary beneficiary.

A corporate trustee was initially appointed for the four trusts, which at time of the marriage was Keach Nominees Pty Ltd. The father held five shares and the mother and the children (including the husband) held one share each. The father was the principal of the Junior Trust.

Keach Nominees Pty Ltd retired as trustee of the Junior Trust and was replaced by J Pty Ltd, in which the husband's brothers (but not the husband) were issued one ordinary share each.

The court considered the following:[33]

> '... [the husband's father] established the Junior Trust, ... was the sole source of the assets, at all times ... gave any necessary legal instructions to the Trust's solicitors, the accounts of the Trust were managed by an accountant under the direction of the ... father ... who at all times ... managed and controlled the Trust, any assistance [the father] received in that regard from the husband was always under [the father's] direction ... and he determined what assets the Trust would hold and acquire ... attended the auction and bid for the M property ... arranged the finances for the purchase by the Trust of the property ... It is also noteworthy that not all allocations/distributions of the income of the Trust were made to the husband. The wife's senior counsel suggested that the evidence of this is incomplete, and it was not possible to determine the full extent of the allocations/distributions. However, I do not accept that submission. There is ample evidence to demonstrate the pattern of allocations/distributions and they certainly were not all to the husband. Indeed, it was the opposite. There were only four allocations/distributions of income to him over a period of 23 years. I also find that the wife was under no illusion as to the ownership of the property. I consider that

she was aware that the Trust owned the property from the time of its purchase …'

Accordingly, the court held that the assets of the Junior Trust should not form part of the property pool and should be treated as a financial resource only.

Although prior to the *Kennon v Spry decision*, the case of *Webster & Webster*[34] is relevant in this context as the husband sought to argue that the trusts in question were the 'alter ego' of the wife, and should be included in the property pool.

The facts are as follows:

(1) the wife was originally a beneficiary of a family trust established by the wife's (late) father. On the wife's 40th birthday, according to a letter of wishes drafted by the father, the capital of the trust was to be distributed to the wife (and any of her children in such proportions as the trustees thought fit);
(2) at the same time as the distribution, two trusts were established, being the P Trust and the Q Trust, to receive the assets from the original trust;
(3) the wife was the appointor of both trusts;
(4) the wife, the wife's mother, the children and remoter issue of the wife and any spouse of the children and remoter issue were listed as income and capital beneficiaries of the P Trust;
(5) the beneficiaries of the Q Trust were the wife, her children and remoter issue and their spouses; and
(6) the wife was the sole director of the corporate trustee of both trusts.

During the proceedings, the wife offered an undertaking to the court and the husband (which the court accepted) to:[35]

'... not at any time in the future exercise, cause or permit to be exercised any position or power under the Deed dated 11 July 1996 establishing the trust known as the Q Trust which would have the effect of causing or permitting any distribution to be made to any potential beneficiary other than the said children.'

The trial judge held that establishing a trust for the protection of the children had been one of the objectives to achieve the wishes of the wife's father. To this effect the trial judge held:[36]

'So while the husband's original intention appeared to accord with the wife's, by the case presented on his behalf he now seeks to shift from that by having his entitlement determined by treating the funds as owned by the wife absolutely. Of course it is the fact that the funds have been lent to ... entities, this has been done on an interest free basis and the wife, therefore, as the beneficial owner of the entities concerned has the use and benefit of the whole of the funds in her current operations. Provided that is recognised, I can see no cause to ignore the intention (initially at least shared by the husband) to benefit the children when the Trust was created and, in the light of the undertaking offered by the wife, no reason to set aside or ignore the rights and obligations created at that time by the Trust. Accordingly, it is proper, in my opinion, to view this fund not as an asset of the wife's but as a resource available to her, indeed a substantial one.

... Whether the assets of any trust are to be included in the assets available for distribution is a matter of fact to be determined taking into account various considerations. More often than not the assets of discretionary trusts are included in the net asset pool because the factual analysis suggests they ought to be. But there is no automatic assumption or presumption that they be treated this way as distinct from constituting a resource to the controlling party. Here in this case, the facts suggest that the trust was indeed specifically established for the children's benefit and protection, that was done consciously as part of the arrangements in re-settling the [original] Trust, it was a step which clearly had the support not only of the wife but also the husband at the time. That ought to be respected now.'

The Full Court upheld the earlier judgment, stating that:[37]

'... given that it was the intention of both the husband and the wife that the children would have an interest in the property or income of the trust ... it was open to the trial Judge, in the somewhat unusual circumstances of this case, to conclude that the trust property should be taken into account in the proceedings as a financial resource of the wife and not as her property ... In so doing, the trial Judge ... was not excluding the assets held by the Trust from her consideration. We are thus not satisfied that the ground of not finding as a fact that the Q Trust was the alter ego of the wife and treating its assets as a resource rather than as assets immediately available to the wife has been established and it is not necessary for us to determine whether, in the circumstances of this case, the trial Judge erred in accepting the undertaking given by the wife.'

The case of *Leader & Martin-Leader*[38] considered a scenario where neither party to the relationship had control of the trust assets. In this case, the wife was listed as a discretionary beneficiary of several trusts established by the wife's parents.

The wife was one of seven parties to a family agreement which catalogued that the wife and her siblings were within the definition of an eligible beneficiary for a number of trusts. Under the agreement, the siblings acknowledged that 'although they qualified as beneficiaries' under particular trusts, they agreed to direct the trustee not to consider them (or any spouse or descendent) when exercising its discretion to distribute income or capital from the relevant trust fund.[39]

In light of this, the court held:[40]

'Similarly, whether the interest of the wife as a person within a class of beneficiaries is to be described as 'property' or a 'financial resource' is a matter which can only be determined after the full consideration of all of the relevant evidence which has been provided and appropriately tested

...

> On the face of the documents produced and the evidence ... it appears that the ultimate control of the trusts and entities under consideration remains with the wife's parents.
>
> Thus, the related factors of control by one party to the marriage and a potential beneficial interest of one party to the marriage which existed together in the matter of *Kennon v Spry* (supra) can be distinguished from this matter in which it is asserted that the wife does not have any control of any of the entities but is merely a potential beneficiary or a person falling within the class of beneficiaries. The Family Agreement between the parents and siblings is not construed to be binding upon the parents so far as their exercise of control of the trust is concerned. The Family Agreement could be construed as providing the wife with certain rights in relation to her siblings and possible other rights yet to be determined.
>
> The decision of Kennon v Spry (supra) dealt specifically with consideration of issues relating to what was property of the husband and wife or parties to the marriage. The decision did not consider whether the entitlements of either of the parties could be described as a financial resource and thus relevant for the purposes of ss 75(2) and 79 of the Family Law Act.
>
> In this case the wife's status as a potential beneficiary or a person who could be described as an 'eligible beneficiary' is a factor which may be relevant to determining the financial resources of the wife ...'

In *Edgehill & Edgehill*,[41] the wife's mother established a discretionary trust and appointed the wife as trustee and a class B beneficiary with the wife's children. The wife's two siblings were class A and C beneficiaries respectively.

Shortly after separation from the husband:

(1) the wife was removed as a trustee and beneficiary; and
(2) the wife's mother prepared a memorandum of wishes of which it was held part of its purposes were:[42]

> '... that on her death the trustees of the trust may, if the trustee acts on her wishes, re-settle the family trust into three discretionary trusts for the benefit of each of her children, grandchildren and their lineal descendants.'

The court held that the interest was a financial resource not property and, in particular, the trial judge made the following comments:[43]

> 'There are a whole range of possibilities attaching to the ultimate benefit which the wife may receive under this trust. The recent documentation relating to the trust outlining the intention and/or request of the wife's mother in respect of how the trust should be dealt with in the future all seem to me to require the consensus of considerable number of people and having regard to human nature there would have to be, in the absence of clear evidence to the contrary, a probability that there will be a distribution under the trust some time (probably within two or three years) of the demise of the wife's mother.'

Source of trust assets

As part of the property settlement process, it is relevant to consider the contributions made by each of the parties to creating the relationship property. In this context, the courts normally place at least some weight on the source of assets owned via a trust.

In *Simmons & Simmons*,[44] the wife argued that the husband's interest in the trust should be included in the property pool. The relevant trust was a discretionary trust settled by the husband's father in 1979. All of the members of the husband's family were potential beneficiaries.

The court found that there was a sufficient nexus between the husband and the trust in that he had significantly invested in the trust by personally making loans to the trust. This, in the court's opinion, was sufficient to consider the assets of the trust to be included as the property of the parties to the marriage.

Similarly, in Pittman & Pittman,[45] a trust was established with the husband listed as a general and specified beneficiary, together with his father, his mother and siblings.

The husband's father (who was the appointor and guardian of the trust on its establishment) nominated the husband's mother, the husband and his brothers, as appointors and guardians after his death. Under two later deeds, the trust fund was irrevocably appointed in favour of the nominated beneficiaries in equal shares (which included the husband).

The court held as follows:[46]

> 'We consider that the PFT interest was property because whatever the original nature of that trust and the husband's interest in it, the various amending instruments have resulted in a situation where the husband has irrevocable entitlements not only to income, but also to a share of capital.

It is true that there is a possibility (perhaps best described as a theoretical possibility) that the husband's one quarter share of the capital might ultimately be diluted by the appointment of other beneficiaries. But he would still be entitled to some share in the capital. It is only the value of his share that might change (indeed it might increase on his mother's death).

The values of all items of property which are the subject of section 79 proceedings are likely to change between the time of such proceedings and the time when such items are eventually realised. Uncertainty of ultimate value cannot provide a reason for not categorising an item as property, and the submissions of Senior Counsel for the husband to the contrary must be rejected.

We also reject the submissions of Senior Counsel for the husband which sought to rely on the absence of control in the husband over the trust.

It is true that the husband cannot be said to have control of the trust, but that fact does not affect his irrevocable entitlements to a quarter of the income of the trust and to a share in the capital.'

While both of these cases are examples where trust assets were treated as property of the marriage as opposed to merely a financial resource, they also demonstrate the requirement for there to be a significant level of control and nexus to support this conclusion.

Trusts established under an estate plan

ALTHOUGH THE DECISION of *Ward v Ward*[47] was prior to Kennon v Spry, it is important because it was one of the first to consider the application of the court's powers to a modern testamentary discretionary trust (TDT) established under a will.

The parties had a 30-year marriage before their divorce, which produced two children. The court was required to adjudicate a numbers of issues, one of which was how to treat the husband's interest in a TDT.

The will of the husband's mother established a TDT and it was admitted that the dominant purpose in establishing the trust was to protect the husband's inheritance. The trustees of the TDT were the husband's two sisters. The range of beneficiaries included the husband and his two children, but not the wife.

An earlier draft of the mother's will had included the husband as a co-trustee and executor, but she had amended it shortly before her death to exclude the husband from these roles once she became aware of the husband's marriage difficulties.

At the time of the proceedings, by the court's acknowledgment, there was no evidence of any expectations or distributions under the TDT to any of the beneficiaries.

The court found the circumstances as being similar to the matter of Bonnici & Bonnici,[48] in which the Full Court had stated that 'property does not fall into a protected category merely because it is an inheritance'.[49]

The court acknowledged that it was probable that the husband would receive the whole entitlement of the TDT at some point. Despite this, it was held that the interest of the TDT could not be considered property of the husband. Accordingly, the court found that the interest was merely ordinary trust law principles when dealing with trust assets in a property settlement.

As with any court decision, the outcome in relation to a particular trust will often depend on the exact facts and surrounding circumstances. However, arguably the recent decisions indicate that each of the a financial resource of the husband and one that the wife had contributed very little to creating.

> '... any trust structuring steps should be considered and implemented as part of a comprehensive review ...'

The recent decision of *Lovine & Connor*[50] considered the assets in two TDTs (which were administered as one TDT) established in the husband's father's will approximately nine years before the separation of the parties.

The court found the following facts:[51]

(1) the beneficiaries of the TDTs included the husband, his two sisters, and their respective children;
(2) the husband's sisters had each effectively received their one-third interest in the assets of the TDTs;
(3) the remaining assets of the TDTs represented the one-third share of the estate held for the husband, and it was the ultimate intention of the husband to distribute the TDT assets to himself and/or his children; and
(4) the husband was the only real controller of the TDTs and, while the will appointed the husband's sisters as joint trustees with him, they played no active role in the control of the TDT.

The husband argued that the assets of the TDTs should only be classified as a financial resource. However, the trial judge determined (and it was later upheld on appeal[52]) that, due to the husband's control over the assets and the real likelihood that he would ultimately receive the benefit of the assets, the assets of the TDTs should be treated as property of the marriage.[53]

Practical recommendations

IT IS CLEAR from *Kennon v Spry* and subsequent decisions that the Family Court has extremely broad powers beyond following characteristics would tend to lead to a conclusion that trust assets should be considered to be property of the parties to the relationship:

(1) where both spouses are able to benefit, and historically have benefited fully from the income and capital of a trust;
(2) where a spouse is the controller of a trust, for example, as the sole trustee, appointor or through shareholding or directorship of a corporate trustee;
(3) where the property of a trust has been contributed by the parties to the relationship or through the efforts of a party to the relationship; or
(4) the property of the trust was acquired during the relationship.

In light of these broad principles, it is also possible to draw some practical conclusions from the recent court decisions, as outlined below. Many of these principles are particularly relevant when structuring trusts to facilitate the intergenerational transfer of wealth, both during a person's lifetime and under their estate plan.

Obviously, any trust structuring steps should be considered and implemented as part of a comprehensive review, and ideally not immediately prior to a relationship breaking down. As outlined above, *Kennon v Spry* is a clear example of the court's ability to use the powers in s 106B to unwind unilateral changes to a trust once there is evidence that a relationship is starting to strain.

Trust structure audits

Arguably, the overriding principle to apply whenever considering the use of a trust is the appropriate structure of each aspect of the arrangement. The issues that are often relevant in this regard include:

(1) Who is the trustee of the trust? If the trustee ceases to act, do their powers pass to anyone else and, if so, who?
(2) Is the trustee an individual or a company?
(3) If the trustee is a company, who are the directors?
(4) Is there a default distribution of the income and capital of the trust to certain beneficiaries?
(5) Does the trust deed restrict the range of beneficiaries who can receive income or capital distributions?
(6) Does the trustee need consent/ approval of any other person for distribution?
(7) Does the trustee effectively/practically control the trust in an unfettered way?
(8) Does the trustee exercise its powers independently or are they controlled or subject to approval by any other person/entity?
(9) Is the trustee a beneficiary of the trust?
(10) Can a beneficiary or a class of beneficiaries control the actions of the trustee?
(11) Can beneficiaries be removed or added, and if so by whom?
(12) Is there any risk that the trustee may be seen as simply the 'alter ego' of some other person?
(13) Does someone (e.g. an appointor, guardian, principal) have the power to unilaterally change the trustee?
(14) If there is an appointor, is the role automatically terminated on certain events (for example, death, bankruptcy)?
(15) If the appointor ceases to act, do their powers pass to anyone else and, if so, who?
(16) If there is more than one appointor, must they act jointly?
(17) Is the appointor a beneficiary of the trust?
(18) Will the trust own more than one asset class?
(19) For an existing trust, has there been a pattern of income or capital distributions to at risk individuals associated with the trust?

(20) For an existing trust, have there been variations to the deed following establishment that impact on the overall control of the trust?

TDTs

Asset protection strategies and the use of special purpose trusts are important issues to consider in estate planning, particularly where potential beneficiaries are in professional practice occupations or in business, or where there is a risk that a personal relationship of a beneficiary may degenerate in the future. Potential beneficiaries that fall into any of these 'at-risk' categories will be exposed to losing assets, unless appropriate structures are put in place.

A TDT is simply a trust established pursuant to a will. Generally, TDTs are seen as particularly useful in the following circumstances:

(1) to ensure concessional tax treatment is available to distributions of capital and income to minor beneficiaries;
(2) to protect accumulated wealth from wastrel or spendthrift beneficiaries;
(3) to provide for infant children and disabled beneficiaries; and
(4) to help protect inheritances from attack by the Family Law Courts and trustees in bankruptcy.

Often, TDTs are structured to limit the range of beneficiaries to 'lineal descendants', whereby the testator restricts the discretionary powers of the trustee so they may only distribute income or capital (or both) to the testator's children and grandchildren, excluding any spouse of the children and/or grandchildren.

A significant attraction of excluding spouses as potential beneficiaries is the perception that it is more difficult for an excluded spouse to argue before the Family Court that the assets of the TDT should be considered as anything other than a financial resource. Recent cases certainly appear to support this view.

When establishing TDTs as part of an estate plan, it is relevant to consider whether a separate TDT should be established for each child, or if all children should effectively share their inheritance jointly via a single TDT.

There are a myriad of issues that should be taken into account when deciding whether to use a single, multiple or 'hybrid' TDT approach. As with many estate planning issues, there is no 'correct' approach, as different factors will be relevant depending on the situation.

Broadly, a single TDT will most likely be preferable if:

(1) some or all of the children are minors. The primary focus in this situation should be on the surviving spouse and therefore it is not ideal to have wealth held across multiple TDTs where the surviving spouse will likely be in control for many years;
(2) the testator has the vision that the children should act as custodians of the wealth for future generations;
(3) the main objective of establishing the TDT is asset protection; and
(4) the nature of the assets (such as a real property) would render a split ownership structure overly complicated.

In contrast, a multiple TDT approach (i.e. a TDT established for the benefit of each child) may be more appropriate, despite probably offering less security on a relationship breakdown, if:

(1) there are different geographical locations of the children;
(2) the relationships between the children is poor. This consideration is important as jointly controlling wealth might further deepen existing rifts between family members;
(3) the risk profiles of each child's investment outlook differ significantly;
(4) the underlying nature of the trust assets make a single TDT impractical, for example, particular assets being earmarked for the sole control of a particular beneficiary; and

(5) there is a desire to implement different control mechanisms for each child (in this context one child may be the sole controller of their trust, whereas another child may require a co-trustee or be wholly excluded from being a trustee).

The hybrid approach combines elements of a single TDT as well as multiple TDTs. Generally, a hybrid approach distributes a set percentage of the estate (or certain assets) to a 'head TDT' of which the control is shared between the various family members and any independent trustees. This head trust will include all lineal descendants as potential beneficiaries.

Sub-TDTs are then created for each child (and their respective spouses and lineal descendants) to which separate assets are gifted. The children will usually control their own sub-TDT and independently regulate succession of the sub-TDT.

Letters of wishes

Another factor that Family Courts have considered relevant, particularly in recent times, is the use of a letter of wishes, which is often prepared by a testator (in the case of a TDT) or significant contributor to a trust.

A letter of wishes is typically a non-binding document that gives guidance to the trustee as to how they should ideally exercise their discretionary powers to administer a trust's assets.

In both *Breakspear & Ackland*[54] and *Read & Chang*,[55] the courts ordered disclosure of the relevant letters of wishes. The predicament specifically considered by Brigg J in *Breakspear & Ackland* was that, on one hand, the disclosure of such confidential documents would cause them to lose favour with those establishing trusts, arguably resulting in less favourable and helpful information for trustees.

Conversely, a letter of wishes is often crucial to determining the manner in which the trustees are likely to exercise their powers. Withholding disclosure may reduce the practical extent to which trustees can be held accountable and courts could make informed decisions about how to factor a trust's assets into a property settlement.

In Read & Chang,[55] Cohen J acknowledged the decision in *White & Tulloch v White*[56] which found that the key criteria to determine if disclosure is appropriate is whether the evidence is, or may be, relevant to the just and equitable process under s 79 of the *Family Law Act* 1975. In particular, the likely relevance will depend upon the nature of the claims being put forward and the overall facts of a particular case[57] or, as the court held:[58]

> 'Although trustees should primarily regard themselves as having a duty to withhold disclosure of a confidential memorandum of wishes ... the Trustees and Court ought determine whether countervailing circumstances, including the likely relevance of the wishes of the person at whose request the trust was created, warrants disclosure.'

Arguably, if trustees are concerned about protecting the confidentiality of letters of wishes, in light of these cases, they should consider advancing no reasons at all for the decision to withhold the letter as, if they do advance such reasons, the court is entitled (upon application by a beneficiary) to enquire as to the reasonableness of the trustee's decision.[59]

Read & Chang[55] in particular demonstrates this point. In that case, the trustees admitted to being influenced by the memorandum of wishes in making past income distributions to the wife from the relevant trust. This admission gave credence to the husband's argument that the letter would better inform the court about future distributions, and the court therefore examined the relevant document before making its decision.

Range of beneficiaries

As noted above, when structuring trusts, careful consideration should always be given to the range of potential beneficiaries and, in particular, whether spouses should be included. Generally, it is difficult for the Family Court to draw a sufficient nexus between a trust and the parties to a relationship where the relevant spouse has never been a beneficiary of the trust.

In the case of *Essex & Essex*,[60] the mere possibility of receiving trust distributions was confirmed as being sufficient to support a finding that the trust was a financial resource. In particular, the court held:[61]

> 'The husband was a named income beneficiary of the S Trust. The husband at no time sought to remove himself as a beneficiary, and the husband's brother's attempt to do so had no relevant purpose (other than to attempt to put the trust's assets beyond the reach of the Court) ... Significantly, as the sole director of the corporate trustee of the S Trust the husband's brother had control of that trust and was only obliged to consider the husband as one of the three income beneficiaries entitled to the income of the trust. However, the husband's brother conceded that, but for a disqualifying factor (the property proceedings) the husband should have the benefit of assets in the trusts. This in our view required the trial Judge to find that the S Trust was a financial resource of the husband.'

Distributions

It is common for parents to use trust assets to assist children with making personal investments, for example, the purchase of a family home. Rather than simply distributing or gifting assets to the relevant child, significant asset protection can be achieved by having funds loaned by the trust, with appropriate security taken over the assets acquired by the child.

Similarly, trust assets can often be inadvertently drawn into the property pool where there are unpaid present entitlements or credit loan accounts owing to a party to the relationship breakdown.

In cases where the trust owes a debt to a spouse, that amount will be included as an asset of the spouse without needing to consider the issues outlined above in relation to the trust.

Binding financial agreements

If increased certainty that trust assets will not be exposed in a property settlement is desired, consideration should be given to implementing a binding financial agreement (BFA). Commentary about how a BFA can be a useful tool to limit the application of the Family Court's powers in relation to trust assets is, however, outside the scope of this article.

Conclusion

Superficially, the outcome of *Kennon v Spry* appears to undermine the fundamental principle of trust law that a mere discretionary beneficiary of a trust does not have a property interest in the assets of the trust. Ultimately, however, the decision is an example of the court's utilisation of the broad powers under the *Family Law Act* in relatively unique circumstances.

While this is an evolving area of law, decisions following *Kennon v Spry* indicate that, for the foreseeable future, well-structured trusts should continue to be an effective vehicle for asset protection and estate planning.

Matthew Burgess, CTA

Acknowledgment

Thank you for the contribution of the co-authors of the original articles. The authors would also like to thank Daniel Fry of Norton & Smailes Lawyers for undertaking the peer review.

This article was originally presented at The Tax Institute's 28th National Convention, held in Perth on 13 to 15 March 2013.

References

[1] *Australian Securities and Investments Commission; In the Matter of Richstar Enterprises Pty Ltd (ACN 099 071 968) v Carey (No 6)* [2006] FCA 814.

[2] *FCT v Bamford* [2010] HCA 10.

[3] *Colonial First State Investments Ltd v FCT [2011] FCA* 16.

[4] *FCT v David Clark; FCT v Helen Clark [2011] FCAFC* 5.

[5] Marriage in this article is used to describe all various life spouse relationships; however, references to the sections of the Family Law Act 1975 (Cth) relate only to marriage

[6] [2008] HCA 56.

[7] A MacDonald, 'Protecting the family assets (trust and divorce)', 2010.

[8] K Schurgott, 'Trusts — a brave new world (trusts and asset protection best practice), 2011.

[9] S 4 of the *Family Law Act* 1975 *(Cth)*.

[10] *Kennon v Spry [2008] HCA* 56 *at [54]*.

[11] S 5 of the *Bankruptcy Act* 1966 *(Cth)*.

[12] John David 'Jodee' Rich, while a director of failed Telco One.Tel, transferred his interest in a Sydney harbourside house to his estranged wife hours before One.Tel's insolvency. Allegedly, Mr Rich remained living in the property after the transfer.

[13] *Australian Securities and Investments Commission & Rich [2003] FamCA* 114 *at [114]-[118]*.

[14] A Macdonald, 'Protecting the family assets (trust and divorce)', 2010.

[15] [2007] FamCA 200.

[16] A Davies and S Savini, 'Family law, tax and family breakdown Part 3: Case study – Keach & Keach and Ors [2011] FamCA 192', 2011.

[17] [2011] FamCAFC 245. This case summary has been adapted from the articles by M Burgess and T Lucke published by Thomson Reuters in the 2012 *Weekly Tax Bulletin* 48 *at [1750], and by M Burgess and J Ford published by Thomson Reuters in the* 2012

Weekly Tax Bulletin 39 *at [1586].*

[18] S 90AE(2)(a) of the *Family Law Act* 1975 *(Cth).*

[19] S 90AF(1) of the *Family Law Act* 1975 *(Cth).*

[20] S 90AF(2) of the *Family Law Act* 1975 *(Cth).*

[21] [2009] FamCAFC 240.

[22] *Stephens & Stephens (Enforcement) [2009] FamCAFC 240 at [355].*

[23] *Beeson & Spence [2007] FamCA 200 at [28].*

[24] [2012] FamCA 30. This case summary has been adapted from the article by M Burgess and J Ford published by Thomson Reuters in the 2012 *Weekly Tax Bulletin* 34 *at [1373].*

[25] *Morton & Morton [2012] FamCA 30 at [35].*

[26] *Harris & Harris [2011] FamCAFC 245.*

[27] *Harris & Harris [2011] FamCAFC 245 at [65]-[67].*

[28] [2009] FamCAFC 236.

[29] *Essex & Essex (No.2) [2007] FamCA 639 at [124].*

[30] *Essex & Essex [2009] FamCAFC 236 at [172]*

[31] *Essex & Essex [2009] FamCAFC 236 at [154].*

[32] [2011] FamCA 192.

[33] *Keach & Keach [2011] FamCA 192 at [172.21]- [172.23].*

[34] [1998] FamCA 1517.

[35] *Webster & Webster [1998] FamCA 1517 at [56].*

[36] *Webster & Webster [1998] FamCA 1517 at [104].*

[37] *Webster & Webster [1998] FamCA 1517 at [109]-[110].*

[38] [2009] FamCA 979.

[39] *Leader & Martin-Leader [2009] FamCA 979 at [24].*

[40] *Leader & Martin-Leader* [2009] FamCA 979 at [74]-[80].

[41] [2007] FamCA 1102.

[42] *Edgehill & Edgehill [2007] FamCA* 1102 *at [82].*

[43] *Edgehill & Edgehill [2007] FamCA* 1102 *at [22].*

[44] [2008] FamCA 1088.

[45] [2010] FamCAFC 30.

[46] *Pittman v Pittman [2010] FamCAFC* 30 *at [63]-[65].*

[47] *Ward & Ward [2004] FMCAfam* 193.

[48] [1992] FLC ¶92-272.

[49] [2004] FMCAfam 193 at [30].

[50] [2011] FamCA 432.

[51] *Lovine & Connor [2011] FamCA* 432 *at [122]-[123], [126].*

[52] *Lovine & Connor [2012] FamCAFC* 168.

[53] *Lovine & Connor [2011] FamCA* 432 *at [121]-[123], [126].*

[54] [2008] EWHC 220 (Ch).

[55] [2010] FamCA 876.

[56] (1995) 19 Fam LR 696.

[57] *Read & Chang [2010] FamCA* 876 *at [7].*

[58] *Read & Chang [2010] FamCA* 876 *at [28].*

[59] S Collins, S Kempster, M McMillan, A Meek (eds), *International trust disputes, Oxford University Press,* 2012.

[60] *Essex & Essex [2009] FamCAFC* 236.

[61] *Essex & Essex [2009] FamCAFC* 236 *at [176]-[177].*

FAILED TRUST DISTRIBUTIONS: THEIR TAX CONSEQUENCES

Failed trust distributions: their tax consequences

Abstract:

THERE IS A range of issues that can potentially undermine the intentions of a trustee when attempting to make distributions from the trust to beneficiaries. Failure to address methodically each potential issue in a timely way will lead to unintended outcomes that may be impossible to remedy once discovered. Further, there is increasing evidence that the Australian Taxation Office is acutely aware of many of the issues, and actively conducts compliance activity in the area. This article focuses on a number of the more common scenarios where purported distributions fail, in the context of a typical family discretionary trust with a range of beneficiaries, including family members and related trusts and companies. It also addresses the potential resulting tax consequences. The article considers trust distributions to a 'beneficiary', distributions to particular beneficiaries, ATO requirements for tracing distributions, areas of ATO focus, and the ramifications of failed distributions.

Introduction

A methodical approach is needed when approaching trust distributions to ensure that the intended outcomes are achieved. This article focuses on a number of the more common scenarios where purported distributions fail. It also addresses the potential resulting tax consequences.

Unless otherwise flagged, all references to trusts in this article should be read as a reference to a 'typical' family discretionary trust with a range of beneficiaries, including a wide range of family members and related trusts and companies.

The specific scenarios considered in this article broadly follow the topics and order set out under the following specific headings:

(1) trust distributions to a 'beneficiary';
(2) distributions to particular beneficiaries;
(3) Australian Taxation Office (ATO) requirements for tracing distributions;
(4) areas of ATO focus; and
(5) ramifications of failed distributions.

Trust distributions to a 'beneficiary'

Is the intended recipient a beneficiary?

A BENEFICIARY IS A person or an entity who has an equitable interest in the trust fund. A potential beneficiary has enforceable rights against a trustee who fails to comply with their duties.

The range of eligible beneficiaries will generally be defined in the trust deed, and the first step in any proposed distribution should be to ensure that the intended recipient falls within the range of potential beneficiaries of the trust.

The Federal Court, from a tax perspective, confirmed in *Yazbek v FCT*[1] that a beneficiary is not simply a person who, as a matter of fact, has obtained some tangible benefit from the trust, but rather they are someone 'who is entitled to enforce the trustee's obligation to administer the trust according to its terms'. In other words, a person is a beneficiary if they fall within the range of eligible beneficiaries under the trust deed, regardless of whether they have ever received distributions of income or capital from the trust.

When considering whether an intended recipient is an eligible beneficiary, care should be taken to identify classes of specifically excluded beneficiaries, which will typically override the provisions in a trust deed which create the class of potential beneficiaries. Some common examples of these excluded classes include:

(1) persons who have either renounced their beneficial interest or have been removed as a beneficiary of the trust fund;
(2) the settlor;
(3) any 'notional settlor' (discussed below); and
(4) the trustee.

A comprehensive review of a trust deed must include an analysis of every variation or resolution of a trustee or other person that may impact on the interpretation of the document.

The range of documents that could impact on the potential beneficiaries of a trust at any particular point in time is almost limitless. Some examples include:

(1) resolutions of the trustee to add or remove beneficiaries pursuant to a power in the trust deed;

(1) nominations or decisions of persons nominated in roles such as a principal, an appointor or a nominator; and

(2) consequential changes triggered by the way in which the trust deed is drafted (for example, beneficiaries who are only potential beneficiaries while other named persons are living).

It is important to remember that the unilateral actions of a potential beneficiary may also impact on whether they can validly receive a distribution. For example, a named beneficiary may disclaim their entitlement to a distribution in any particular year, or may in fact renounce all interests under the trust.

There are a myriad of issues that potentially arise in relation to disclaimers and renunciation that are outside the scope of this article. This said, the fact that beneficiaries can unilaterally take such steps highlights the care that trustees must take when determining whether an intended recipient of a distribution is in fact a valid beneficiary of the trust.

In most instances within a close family group, the trustee is likely to have personal knowledge of any changes to the range of eligible beneficiaries (such as a unilateral renunciation by a beneficiary). However, these changes will not always be apparent to a professional adviser whose knowledge is limited to the trust documentation provided to them.

Inappropriately appointed beneficiaries

To the extent that steps have been taken to nominate additional beneficiaries, an analysis is needed as to whether the nomination was effective pursuant to the trust deed.

An example of a clause in a trust deed defining the range of beneficiaries and permitting additional beneficiaries to be appointed is as follows:

'Additional Members of the Class of General Beneficiaries:

a The children of the Primary Beneficiaries;
b The more remote issue of the Primary Beneficiaries including any grandchildren or any Trust which may be formed for any of them or for any of the Primary beneficiaries;
c Any company in which any one or more of them may hold a controlling interest; and
d Any person, trustee or company who shall be entitled by nomination of the appointor to become a general beneficiary.'

Given the way in which this clause is crafted, if there is an intention to distribute to a beneficiary not otherwise clearly within the parameters of subparas (a) to (c), then the strict requirements of subparagraph (d) must be followed and the intended beneficiary must be formally nominated by the appointor.

Obviously, there are a number of potential issues that arise in this regard, including:

(1) whether the appointment needs to be made in writing;
(2) whether the appointor is validly nominated in their role;
(3) at what point the nomination needs to take place in the context of the time frame within which a distribution must be made; and
(4) whether there are any consequential ramifications of the nomination, for example, stamp duty, resettlement for tax purposes or asset protection issues.

None of these issues should be considered in isolation and must be addressed methodically by the trustee and their advisers.

Exclusion of settlor: the notional settlor clause

Almost all trust deeds contain a clause excluding the settlor of a trust from being a beneficiary in order to ensure that the trust is not a 'revocable trust' under s 102 of the Income Tax Assessment Act 1936 (Cth) (ITAA36). Some deeds, however, take the restriction further by prohibiting distributions to any 'notional settlor', in addition to the actual settlor. For example, a trust deed may include a provision along the following lines:

> 'A person who has transferred property for other than full consideration in money or money's worth to the Trustee to be held as an addition to the Trust Fund (herein called 'the excluded persons'), or any corporation in which and the trustee of any settlement or trust in or under which any excluded person has an actual or contingent beneficial interest, so long as such interest continues, is excluded from the class of General Beneficiaries.'

Where such a clause exists, a beneficiary will likely be excluded from receiving distributions if they have:

(1) made interest-free loans to the trust;
(2) sold an asset to the trust at less than market value; or
(3) gifted cash or other assets to the trust.

As the main beneficiaries of a trust will have often contributed amounts to a trust in one or more of the ways mentioned above, the risk of invalid distributions being made where such a clause exists in a deed are significant and anecdotally we understand that this issue is one the ATO reviews regularly.

Furthermore, any income or capital distributions to a trust (containing a clause along the lines outlined above) from another discretionary trust in the group could be considered a 'transfer of property for other than full consideration'. This would then prevent the trust with the 'notional settlor' clause distributing to those other entities which have previously distributed income or capital to it.

Exclusion of trustee

Another commonly overlooked clause relates to the exclusion of the trustee, be that the current, former or future trustee, as a beneficiary of the trust. These clauses are often found in deeds prepared by New South Wales advisers, as s 54(3) of the Duties Act 1997 (NSW) limits the nominal duty exemption for a change of trustee to trust deeds that contain provisions ensuring:

(1) none of the continuing trustees remaining after the appointment of a new trustee are or can become a beneficiary under the trust;
(2) none of the trustees of the trust after the appointment of a new trustee are or can become a beneficiary under the trust; and
(3) the transfer is not part of a scheme for conferring an interest, in relation to the trust property, on a new trustee or any other person, whether as a beneficiary or otherwise, to the detriment of the beneficial interest or potential beneficial interest of any person.

An example of such a clause complying with the above is as follows:

'None of the continuing Trustees remaining after the retirement of a Trustee is or can become a beneficiary under the Trust, and none of the Trustees of the Trust after the appointment of a new Trustee is or can become a beneficiary under the Trust.'

As with all of the previous clauses, the impact of this type of restriction will ultimately depend on how the clause is drafted in the relevant trust deed.

Distributing to a non-beneficiary

THE CASE OF *Harris v Harris*[2] considered the purported distributions from a trust to a recipient who was found not to be a beneficiary. On reading the trust deed for the family trust, the trial judge noted that the recipient in question was not in fact an eligible beneficiary of the trust. This meant, in the context of the case and for the purposes of a property settlement, the recipient should be ignored as a beneficiary as all of the potential value derived was from invalid distributions.

While the 'wrongful distributions' (in the words of the court) were not explored further, the decision highlights the importance of reading the source documentation before any steps are taken to rely on what might otherwise be assumed to be permitted.

Where a distribution has been made to an excluded beneficiary, a range of tax and commercial issues arise. Again, a detailed analysis of the various ramifications in this regard is outside the scope of this article; however, briefly:

(1) whether there are valid default distribution provisions under a trust deed will be highly relevant;

(2) the effectiveness of any default distribution clause needs to be carefully considered, as highlighted in the BRK case (summarised in more detail below);

(3) a significant number of trust deeds will either have no default provisions or the default provisions will be ineffective; and

(4) where there are no default provisions, at least in relation to capital, there is a risk that the trust itself will be considered void.

Assuming that there is a valid default distribution provision which operates as intended, the main consequences are commercial in nature. In particular, the practicalities that surround recovery of invalid trust distributions, reallocation of the distributions, together with the flow-on taxation and stamp duty implications and potential personal liability for the trustee.

These issues are all also relevant if there is no valid default distribution provision. However, where that situation arises, the trustee is assessed under s 99A ITAA36 on the basis that no beneficiary will be presently entitled. This means that the trustee is assessed at the top marginal tax rate of 45% plus the Medicare levy of 1.5%, unless the Commissioner exercises his discretion in the limited circumstances specified in s 99A(2) ITAA36.

Importantly, where the trustee is taxed under s 99A ITAA36, the ability to access the general 50% capital gains tax discount is denied.

Family trust elections and interposed entity elections

IN ADDITION TO the traditional trust law-related restrictions on the potential beneficiaries of a trust, it is important to keep in mind the consequences of a trustee making a family trust election or interposed entity election. In particular, where such an election has been made, despite what might otherwise be provided for in the trust instrument, the election will effectively limit the range of potential beneficiaries who can receive a distribution without triggering a penal tax consequence (being the family trust distribution tax).

A family trust election will generally be made by a trustee for one or more of the following reasons:

(1) access to franking credits;
(2) ability to utilise prior year losses and bad debt deductions;
(3) simplifying the continuity of ownership test; and
(4) eliminating the need to comply with the trustee beneficiary reporting rules (as mentioned in more detail below).

A family trust election is made in accordance with s 272-80 of Sch 2F ITAA36 which requires that a 'test individual' be specified, of which their family will benefit from all future distributions.

A test individual's family will broadly include, under s 272-95 of Sch 2F ITAA36, the immediate family of the test individual and their spouse, as well as the lineal descendants of the immediate family.

Once a family trust election has been made, the trust will be restricted to making distributions to trust beneficiaries within the family group. Failure to do so will incur family trust distribution tax being imposed at a flat rate of 47%, which is payable by the distributing trust within 21 days after distribution is made.

Likewise, an interposed entity election for a company, trust or partnership in a test individual's family group may be made where income is intended to be distributed to that entity from a trust that has a family trust election in place. In order to be eligible to make an interposed entity election, a 'family control test' must be satisfied, as set out under s 272-87 of Sch 2F ITAA36.

Again, while a full analysis of the impact of family trust elections and interposed entity elections is outside the scope of this article, it is critical to consider the potential implications of any such election on what might otherwise appear to be a permissible distribution in accordance with the trust deed.

Practical application

SET OUT BELOW are some clauses extracted from a 'standard' trust deed established in the 1990s. The provisions highlight how some of the issues outlined above can arise when determining whether intended trust distributions are likely to be effective.

Deed provisions

The beneficiaries were defined in the trust deed as follows:

'The Primary Beneficiaries means that person or persons specified as such in the Schedule hereto.

The Secondary Beneficiaries means the person or persons specified as such in the Schedule hereto.

The Tertiary Beneficiaries means the person or persons specified as such in the Schedule hereto.

The Primary Beneficiaries, the Secondary Beneficiaries and the Tertiary Beneficiaries include persons who from time to time until the Perpetuity Date come under each category respectively notwithstanding that such persons may not be in existence, or have not come into such category at the date of this Deed.'

The beneficiaries were listed in the schedule of the trust deed as follows:

'Primary Beneficiaries:

a Joseph Jones;
b Janet Jones;
c the children of the said Joseph Jones and the said Janet Jones; and

d the grandchildren of the said Joseph Jones and the said Janet Jones.

Secondary Beneficiaries:

a the parents of the said Joseph Jones;
b the brothers and sisters of the said Joseph Jones; and
c the children of the brothers and sisters of the said Joseph Jones.

Tertiary Beneficiaries:

a the parents of the said Janet Jones;
b the brothers and sisters of the said Janet Jones; and
c the children of the brothers and sisters of the said Janet Jones.'

The following clause in the trust deed provided the power to appoint additional beneficiaries:

'Notwithstanding anything to the contrary herein contained the Trustee shall have the power at any time or times and from time to time in its absolute discretion with or without consideration to pay, transfer, apply, set aside or accumulate the whole or any part of the Trust Fund and/or income to any such persons, incorporated companies, trusts, charities, bodies or associations whether incorporated or unincorporated having a separate legal identity in the country or place according to the laws of which they have been created as the Principal during his, her or their lifetime shall by notice in writing to the Trustee before the Perpetuity Date appoint to be a beneficiary for the purpose of this Deed PROVIDED HOWEVER and notwithstanding the provisions of anything herein contained or implied none of the following shall be appointed to be a beneficiary nor they shall be permitted to acquire a beneficial interest in the Income or capital of the Trust or any part thereof

a the Settlor; or
b a Trustee or former Trustee hereof; or
c any corporation or Trust in which the settlor or any Trustee or former Trustee has any actual or contingent beneficial interest;

or

d any Trust which would, if appointed, result in the infringement of the law against perpetuities.

PROVIDED FURTHER that where the primary beneficiaries or any one or more of them (not being a body corporate) shall be the original Trustee hereof the provisions of this clause shall not apply in respect of any payment, transfer, application, setting aside or accumulation hereunder by the Trustee to such primary beneficiary nor to the acquisition of a beneficial interest in the income or capital of the trust or any part thereof by such primary beneficiary from the Trustee.

The expressions 'beneficiary', 'beneficiaries',

'Beneficiary' or 'Beneficiaries' where used in this Deed or in the Schedule hereto shall include beneficiaries appointed pursuant to the terms of [this clause].'

Relevantly, the variation clause allowed the trustee to vary the trust deed, subject to the following restrictions:

'... PROVIDED THAT the Trustee shall not have any power to revoke add to or vary any of the trusts or powers hereof so that the Settlor or the Trustee may acquire a beneficial interest in the Trust Fund or any part thereof nor to affect the beneficial entitlement of any Beneficiary to any amount applied for him prior to the date or revocation or alteration ...'

More importantly:

(1) the initial trustee was Joseph Jones; and
(2) the initial principal was Janet Jones.

Factual scenario

Over a period of some years, the following additional events took place (among other things):

(1) the original trustee was replaced with a corporate trustee;
(2) the corporate trustee was used as a corporate beneficiary of the trust; and
(3) distributions were made to Joseph Jones.

Practical implications

The first time the trust deed was comprehensively reviewed in relation to the history of distributions was as part of proceedings brought by the former daughter-in-law of Joseph and Janet Jones, who was (among other things) arguing that her husband (one of the sons of Joseph and Janet) was entitled, pursuant to the default distribution provisions under the trust, to distributions (plus interest) that had historically been purported to be made to both Joseph Jones and the corporate beneficiary.

Other relevant issues identified as part of the initial review (in the context of the focus of this article) included the following:

(1) in addition to the apparently invalid distributions to Joseph Jones and the corporate beneficiary, there were obviously also consequential limitations on distributions to related entities;
(2) while the breadth of excluded beneficiaries may have been wider than initially intended, the specific prohibition on variations to the trust deed would seem to prevent any steps that may be taken to remove the initial restrictions; and
(3) the records of the trust were also incomplete in relation to the written notification by the principal nominating certain additional beneficiaries.

Distributions to particular beneficiaries

REGARDLESS OF WHETHER a distribution is otherwise permissible, there are a number of particular types of distributions that should be carefully considered before they are made. The three most relevant categories in this regard are as follows:

(1) trust-to-trust distributions;
(2) distributions to non-resident beneficiaries; and
(3) distributions to companies.

Each of these distributions is considered below.

Distributions from trust to trust

All Australian jurisdictions except for South Australia have a statutory perpetuity period of 80 years. In Victoria, Tasmania, Western Australia and the Northern Territory, the common law perpetuity period may also be adopted, that is, 'a life in being plus 21 years'.

Despite South Australia essentially abolishing the rule against perpetuities, s 62 of the *Law of Property Act 1936* (SA) allows the court to dispose of any remaining unvested interests after 80 years on the application of a beneficiary.

Generally, when trust-to-trust distributions are made, the vesting date of both trusts should be considered. Where the recipient has a vesting date which is later than the distributing trust, the risk that the rule against perpetuities is breached is a relevant issue.

Historically, many advisers believed that, if the vesting date of the recipient trust was later than the distributing trust, then this automatically caused a breach of the rule against perpetuities, making the purported distribution void. However, the case of *Nemesis Australia*

Pty Ltd (formerly Steve Hart Family Holdings Pty Ltd) v FCT[3] confirmed that the 'wait and see rule' in s 210 of the Property Law Act 1974 (Qld) can be relied on in a situation where a trust distributes to another trust with a later perpetuity date.

The 'wait and see' rule means that the initial distribution will not be void when made, and will not become void until such time as there is a failure to distribute out of the recipient trust before the vesting date of the original distributing trust.

Distributions from trust to non-resident beneficiary

When making trust distributions to non-resident beneficiaries, it is important to consider the interaction between s 128A ITAA36 in relation to withholding tax for non-residents and the general provisions of Div 6 ITAA36 in relation to the taxation of trust distributions.

Withholding tax will be payable on all dividends, interest or royalties included in the income paid by a resident trust to a non-resident beneficiary to the extent that the non-resident beneficiary is presently entitled to the relevant amount.

To the extent that income is caught by the withholding tax provisions, s 128D ITAA36 excludes it from being treated as assessable income, which will potentially impact the Div 6 treatment of the relevant trust distributions. For example, if a resident trust distributes income to beneficiaries in the United States (who are non-resident beneficiaries), then:

(1) under the withholding tax system, a flat rate is deducted from the source of the income before the income is sent overseas;
(2) each part of the income (depending on whether it is interest, dividends or royalty distribution) will be taxed on the relevant withholding tax rate, ranging between 10% and 15%; and
(3) if the beneficiary is not presently entitled to the distribution, the withholding tax rules will not take effect.

For trust income distributions to non-residents where withholding tax does not apply, the amount will be taxed to the trustee under s 99 or 99A ITAA36, as outlined earlier in this article.

Distributions from trust to corporate beneficiary

Caution is required when distributing to a corporate beneficiary, in particular if it may result in the creation of an unpaid present entitlement (UPE) owing from a trust to the company.

TR 2010/3 and PS LA 2010/4 outline the ATO's view that it is possible for a Div 7A loan to, in effect, arise from UPEs created after 16 December 2009. Specifically, the Commissioner takes the view in TR 2010/3 that a UPE falls within the 'financial accommodation' definition of a Div 7A loan unless the terms of the arrangement fall within certain safe harbours.

While detailed comments about Div 7A are outside the scope of this article, some of the practical considerations relating to corporate beneficiaries are as follows:

(1) all pre-16 December 2009 UPEs should be 'quarantined' to ensure that they are not treated as Div 7A loans;
(2) trust deeds should be reviewed to ensure that no clauses operate to deem or automatically convert UPEs into loans; and
(3) for post-16 December 2009 trust distributions to corporate beneficiaries, documentation that complies with the Commissioner's stance under TR 2010/3 and PS LA 2010/4 should be implemented (for example, appropriate loan or sub-trust arrangements).

A great deal of literature has been published regarding the accuracy (or otherwise) of the Commissioner's views in TR 2010/3 and PS LA 2010/4, an analysis of which is outside the scope of this article.

ATO requirements for tracing distributions

In addition to the various issues outlined above about the impact that the approach of the ATO has in relation to trust distributions, it is important to remember that trustees will also often have particular reporting requirements imposed on them by the ATO. This is most starkly demonstrated by the requirements of the ATO concerning identification of beneficiaries of certain distributions and, in particular, where trust-to-trust distributions are involved. In this regard, the ITAA36 contains requirements for a trustee to assist the ATO with tracing distributions which have been made to beneficiaries.

Under Div 6D ITAA36, a trustee is required to complete an ultimate beneficiary statement (UBS) where a distribution is made to another trust.

The Commissioner states in PS LA 2001/12 that trustees of a closely held trust group are assumed to know how income is intended to be distributed from the original trust to any recipient trust and finally to the ultimate individual or corporate beneficiary.

By requiring the UBS to be provided, the Commissioner is seeking the ability to easily trace the flow of a distribution through interposed trusts to the ultimate recipients.

Failure to provide the Commissioner with a correct UBS will result in ultimate beneficiary non-disclosure tax being imposed on the trustee of the original trust equal to the highest marginal tax rate plus the Medicare levy (46.5%).

Limited trustee relief from the UBS requirements is available in some situations. PS LA 2001/12 outlines the specific circumstances where relief may be granted, for example, the trustee 'is not in a position to readily identify all ultimate beneficiaries' or is unable to obtain a tax file number from a beneficiary despite otherwise identifying the ultimate beneficiary.

Areas of ATO focus

FOLLOWING THE 2013 federal Budget, the ATO announced the focus of the 'Trusts Taskforce' (Taskforce). In addition to the stated goal of identifying 'egregious tax avoidance and evasion using trust structures', the ATO has said that the Taskforce will examine a number of arrangements, including:

(1) trusts or their beneficiaries who have received substantial income that are not registered, or have not lodged tax returns or activity statements;
(2) offshore dealings involving secrecy jurisdictions;
(3) arrangements which result in income being assessable to low-tax beneficiaries where the benefits of the income are enjoyed by others;
(4) arrangements which involve artificial recharacterisation of amounts to change the tax outcome; and
(5) 'sham' transactions and round-robin circulation of income between related trusts.

The ATO has stated that the intended targets of the Taskforce are high-risk taxpayers and not ordinary arrangements and tax planning associated with genuine business or family dealings.

Ramifications of failed distributions

WHERE A PURPORTED trust distribution is subsequently found to be invalid, there are a series of issues and potential ramifications that may need to be considered. The main issues in this regard include:

(1) the 'knowing recipient' principle;
(2) the impact of disallowed deductions;
(3) disclaimers;
(4) equity and rectification; and
(5) default distribution provisions.

Each of these concepts is dealt with in turn below.

'A comprehensive review of a trust deed must include an analysis of every variation or resolution ...'

Distributions from trustee-knowing recipient

'Knowing recipient' is a principle that evolved out of situations where a trustee (who holds property on trust on behalf of the beneficiaries of a trust) appropriates trust funds for the benefit of a third party who has knowledge of the trust relationship.

The concept gives the 'wronged' beneficiaries the right to make a personal claim against the third party on the basis that the third party received the trust property, while having knowledge of the relationship between the property in question, the trustee and the beneficiary. In other words, the third party knowingly assisted in the wrongful distribution (or breach of trust) by the trustee.

Although the claim is property based, the remedy is personal and it is only available where the third party can be shown to have had knowledge (or ought to have had knowledge) of the breach of trust.

The defences against claims arising from the knowing recipient principle were settled in the case of *Koorootang Nominees Pty v ANZ Banking Group Ltd.*[4]

In that case, it was held that liability should be strict and subject only to the defences of bona fide purchase and change of position.

Effect of disallowed deductions on the trust distribution resolution

The exact manner in which disallowed deductions will be treated turns largely on the way in which the relevant distribution resolution is crafted and, in turn, whether the resolution effectively deals with disallowed deductions. Broadly, there are three possible outcomes, namely:

(1) the amounts representing the disallowed deduction will be validly distributed to a particular beneficiary via the provisions of a distribution resolution;

(2) the default provisions under the trust deed will regulate the distribution; or

(3) the amount will be treated as an accumulation and the trustee will be taxed.

Obviously, where the trustee is taxed, the flat highest marginal tax rate (as explained above) under s 99A ITAA36 will apply.

The case of *Norman and FCT*[5] provides an example of the ramifications of the Commissioner disallowing deductions and the additional amounts being included in the assessable income of a beneficiary due to the way in which the distribution resolution was crafted. In this case, the taxpayer was the director of the corporate trustee for the Norman Family Investment Trust (Norman Trust). The trustee resolved to establish an employee welfare plan which provided for all of the profits of the Norman Trust to be paid to the employees of a related business in the trustee's discretion.

The trustee claimed deductions over a number of years, which the Commissioner subsequently disallowed and imposed tax shortfall penalties of 50% for recklessness on the basis that the employee welfare program was established as a scheme to which the general anti-avoidance provisions of Pt IVA ITAA36 applied.

The Commissioner treated the amounts disallowed as deductions as additional distributions to one of the beneficiaries. The Commissioner's reasoning for this approach was based on the fact that the original resolution of the trustee provided that, after all deductions were properly claimed, any balance of the trust's income should be distributed to that beneficiary. The beneficiary taxpayer objected to this on the basis that the amounts that were now being included in the income of the trust had never in fact been received by them.

The Administrative Appeals Tribunal held that, based on the trustee's resolution regarding the distribution of income, the taxpayer was in fact the person presently entitled and therefore liable for the additional tax, notwithstanding that the amounts in question had never been received by the beneficiary.

Disclaimer and effects on distributions

Arguably, the leading case in relation to disclaimers is *FCT v Ramsden & Ors.*[6] In this case, Steve Hart Family Holdings Pty Ltd (SHF Holdings) was the trustee at all material times of The Steve Hart Family Trust (SHF Trust).

The trust deed of SHF Trust contained a default income clause which provided that the trustee was to hold any undistributed income for the benefit of four named beneficiaries as tenants in common. The named beneficiaries were Troy Hart, Philip Hart, Tamara Ramsden and Steve Hart.

In the year ending 30 June 1996, SHF Holdings as trustee for the SHF Trust prepared a resolution distributing $429,000 to the Adcock Practice Trust (AP Trust), which was neither a general beneficiary, nor an eligible beneficiary.

Among the other trust distributions made by SHF Holdings as trustee for the SHF Trust, no distribution was made to the default beneficiaries named in the trust deed. As a consequence, the named default beneficiaries lodged an income tax return for the year ending 30 June 1996 on the basis that no distribution was received.

In July 2000, the Commissioner issued a notice of amended assessment to each of the named default beneficiaries, increasing their taxable income by $107,250 (i.e. one quarter each of $429,000).

The Commissioner had found that the 1996 distribution of $429,000 to AP Trust was invalid and therefore the default income clause under the trust deed applied.

The four beneficiaries lodged objections to the assessments in September 2000 that were dismissed by the Commissioner. The beneficiaries then appealed against the dismissal to the Federal Court in June 2001.

The default beneficiaries claimed to have disclaimed their interest in the income of the SHF Trust through the following actions:

(1) on 17 April 2002, the beneficiaries claimed to have entered into deeds of disclaimer, disclaiming any amounts (except such amounts paid for their benefit) that may have accrued under the SHF Trust deed for the year ending 30 June 1996;
(2) on 2 October 2003, the beneficiaries confirmed the above disclaimer by signing another set of deeds; and
(3) on 8 October 2003, the beneficiaries entered into additional deeds disclaiming all of their interests to the income of the SHF Trust.

At first instance, Spender J found that the disclaimers made by the beneficiaries were 'effective to disclaim any interest which [they] had in any part of the distribution' of the $429,000. However, on appeal, the Full Federal Court disagreed with the approach of Spender J and held that the disclaimers were ineffective. Specifically, the court found:

(1) that the distribution in favour of AP Trust was a nullity;
(2) that it is possible for a beneficiary to be entitled to more than one gift from a discretionary trust;
(3) when the trustee exercised its discretionary appointment power in accordance with the trust deed, that the gifts made were of a discretionary nature. Moreover, each of these gifts was an independent gift each year and therefore each distribution could be separately disclaimed;
(4) that any interest acquired in the net income of the trust under the default provisions of the deed could be disclaimed by a specified beneficiary separately from any other entitlements which might accrue to that beneficiary under other provisions of the deed;
(5) that, to be effective, a disclaimer under the default provisions of a trust deed must extend to the whole of that subject matter; hence, a purported disclaimer confined to only one accounting period was necessarily ineffective;
(6) that it was accepted that the respondents had knowledge of the interest by April 2001 at the latest; and
(7) that the beneficiaries had to determine, within a reasonable time from the default distribution of April 2001, whether they would renounce the vested interest they had in the annual income of the trust for the duration of the trust. Once they became aware of their vested interests in the trust income, they had to determine in a timely manner whether they wished to disclaim those interests.

It is clear from this decision that a disclaimer can be made with retrospective effect and not simply from the date of the disclaimer, provided it is made within a reasonable period of time from the beneficiary first becoming aware of the relevant interest they wish to disclaim.

Will equity assist a failed distribution?

While equity can assist in relation to a failed trust distribution through rectification, this remedy is only available in limited circumstances.

Broadly, a court may use the equitable remedy of rectification where there is an error requiring correction in a trust document which does not reflect the intentions of the parties and results in a failed or invalid trust distribution.

If rectification is held to be an appropriate remedy, the practical effect is that the document may be changed retrospectively and be able to be read as if it was originally executed in the intended format.

In order for rectification to be granted, the party applying for the court to exercise its discretion must establish three elements:

(1) the intention that the parties had in relation to the document up until the time the distribution resolution was executed;

(2) a mistake was made in the document that does not reflect the parties' true intentions; and

(3) if the rectification order was granted, it would correct the mistake and match the parties' intentions.

A case that highlights the doctrine of rectification being effective for trust distributions is Kirkham as trustee of the Kirkham Family Trust.[7] In this case, Mr Kirkham established a trust under which he was the settlor, the trustee and also a named specific beneficiary.

Due to the way in which the deed was crafted, even though he was a named beneficiary, Mr Kirkham was (under other provisions) excluded from receiving distributions.

Income distributions were made from the trust to Mr Kirkham as if he was an eligible beneficiary as the exclusion was overlooked.

When Mr Kirkham discovered he was not an eligible beneficiary, he applied to the court for rectification so that he would be included as a member of the general beneficiary class. To support his claim for rectification, Mr Kirkham provided the court with evidence that it was his intention as settlor and trustee that he be a beneficiary from the date of the trust deed's execution and that it was a mistake on his solicitor's behalf that he was not included in the general beneficiary class.

Chief Justice Martin held that an order for rectification be granted for Mr Kirkham so that the trust deed was rectified to include Mr Kirkham as a general beneficiary of the trust fund from the date of establishment of the trust. In particular, it was held:

> 'When an application is made for the rectification of a trust instrument the essential question is whether there is clear and convincing evidence that it was the common intention of the settlor and the trustee, at the time the trust was created, that some result other than that which was ultimately effected by the instrument should be achieved.'

The evidence provided by the affidavits of Mr Kirkham, the solicitors who drafted the trust deed and the accountants for the trust established the intention that Mr Kirkham always intended to be included as an eligible beneficiary. That intention was manifested in the fact that Mr Kirkham was nominated expressly as a specified beneficiary in the trust deed and it was also consistent with his actions as trustee in making distributions to companies in which he had an interest.

Ultimately, the court held:

> 'I am satisfied, therefore, that all the appropriate requirements for the making of an order for rectification have been made out. There is clear evidence of the relevant intention of the settlor and the trustee at the time, that intention was frustrated by an accidental omission by those responsible for the preparation of the trust instrument and so the trust instrument did not reflect that intention.'

Although equity may grant rectification in particular circumstances, rectification will not be granted where there is simply an inadvertent financial result. For example, if a party restructures their business for tax advantages based on the advice of an accountant and, after the accountant's advice is followed, large tax liabilities are triggered, rectification is unlikely to be granted.[8]

The key distinction in relation to when a rectification is available is whether the requested correction is concerning a mistake as to the implementation of the parties' intentions as opposed to the ramifications of implementing the arrangements.

Operation of default beneficiary provisions when resolutions fail

As mentioned earlier in this article, one approach designed to prevent the adverse tax consequences that can arise from an invalid distribution could be that discretionary trust deeds will contain default income and capital beneficiary provisions. The purpose of this type of clause is to ensure that, if the trustee fails to effectively exercise their power to distribute trust income or capital, the relevant amount will be automatically distributed to specific beneficiaries who have already been defined in the clause.

An example of this style of provision was illustrated in the case of *Ramsden* (discussed above). That is, although there was an invalid distribution (due to the purported distribution to the AP Trust, which was not in fact a beneficiary), it was ultimately determined that the named specified beneficiaries were entitled.

The main objective from a tax perspective of a default distribution clause is to ensure that the default beneficiaries will be assessed on the failed distribution, rather than the trustee being assessed under s 99A ITAA36 at the top marginal rate.

Care must, however, be taken with the drafting of default clauses that are in fact effective.

The case of BRK (Bris) v FCT[9] is particularly relevant in this regard. In that case, the default distribution clause required that the trustee on default 'divide the Fund equally among the beneficiaries named in the Schedule hereto' on a date after the end of a tax year.

The court held, therefore, that, as the trustee would not in fact make the distribution to the default beneficiaries until after the end of a tax year, the income was accumulated for tax purposes in the previous tax year and, in accordance with s 99A ITAA36, the trustee was taxed on the entire default amount at the top marginal rate.

Care must also be taken to ensure that default clauses are drafted so that the recipient beneficiaries are ascertainable.

The tribunal's findings in *Hopkins & Anor and FCT*[10] are particularly relevant. Specifically, the tribunal considered the certainty as to the objects of the Hopkins Family Trust. The following clauses in relation to the definition of primary beneficiaries, as well as the default income provision, were considered:

> 'The 'Primary Beneficiaries' means and includes RONALD JAMES HOPKINS, KATHLEEN CLARE ADAM, SAMUAL ALAN JOHN HOPKINS, DONNA MAREE HOPKINS, TONY TROY HOPKINS and any other the children and grandchildren, spouses of children and spouses of grandchildren of either of the said RONALD JAMES HOPKINS or the said KATHLEEN CLARE ADAM the parents, brothers and sisters of the said RONALD JAMES HOPKINS and KATHLEEN CLARE ADAM and the children and grandchildren of such brothers and sisters and any company in existence at the Vesting Day incorporated in any country throughout the world the shares in which are owned by any one or more of them or by a Trustee upon trust of any trust or trusts in existence at the Vesting Day under which any one or more of them is a beneficiary present or contingent.
>
> ... the Trustee shall pay or apply the whole or any part of the income in any year of income of the Trust Fund for the benefit of all or such one or more of the Primary Beneficiaries ... PROVIDED that such Deed or oral declaration be made on or before the last day in any year of income and in the event of such Deed or oral declaration not being so made any income not so paid or applied shall be deemed to have been paid or applied for the benefit of the Primary Beneficiaries in equal shares and in such an event the Trustee shall credit such proportions of such income to the account of the respective Primary Beneficiaries in the books of account of the Trustee and shall hold the same absolutely on behalf of each such Primary Beneficiary.'

The tribunal rejected the Commissioner's claim that the there was 'uncertainty in the objects' of the trust and held that, as all of the primary beneficiaries could be ascertained, there being 46 in total, it was possible to say with certainty that 'any given individual was, or was not, a' primary beneficiary of the trust.

Although not explored in the above case, the failure to have a default income clause appropriately drafted would result in the trustee accumulating the default income and taxed under s 99A ITAA36, as explained above.

Conclusion

As highlighted by a number of aspects of this article, there are a range of issues that can potentially undermine the intentions of a trustee when attempting to make distributions.

While the starting point in any situation is always the provisions of the trust deed, trustees must also be acutely aware of a myriad of other potentially relevant issues before making any distribution.

A failure to methodically address each and every potential issue in a timely way will invariably lead to unintended outcomes that, in most instances, will be impossible to remedy once they are discovered. In

this regard, there is increasing evidence to suggest that the ATO is acutely aware of most, if not all, of the issues set out in this article, and actively conducts compliance activity in the area.

Matthew Burgess, CTA

Acknowledgment

Thank you for the contribution of the co-authors of the original articles. The work of Patrick Ellwood, is gratefully acknowledged.

Disclaimer

This article covers legal and technical issues in a general way. It is not designed to express opinions on specific cases. This article is intended for information purposes only and should not be regarded as legal advice. Further advice should be obtained before taking action on any issue dealt with in this publication.

References

[1] [2013] FCA 39.

[2] [2011] FAMCAF 245.

[3](2005) 225 ALR 576.

[4] [1998] 3 VR 16.

[5] [2004] AATA 1164.

[6] [2005] FCAFC 39.

[7] Unreported, Supreme Court of Western Australia, Martin CJ, 19 May 2010.

[8] *Baird v BCE Holdings Pty Ltd* (1996) 40 NSWLR 374.

[9] [2001] FCA 164.

[10] [2012] AATA 324.

FIXED TRUSTS AND UNIT TRUSTS: ONE AND THE SAME?

Fixed trusts and unit trusts: one and the same?

Abstract:

THERE IS SOME uncertainty about what a fixed trust is for taxation purposes. Following the Federal Court decision in *Colonial First State Investments Ltd v FCT* in 2011, it seems that, for taxation purposes, very few traditional unit trusts will satisfy the strict definition of a 'fixed trust'. This article considers the specific requirements for a trust qualifying as a fixed trust and the relevance of the fixed trust concept for taxation purposes. Specifically, this article examines whether fixed trusts and unit trusts are the same, unit trusts and franked dividends, the status of distributions that are not fixed, borrowing by unit trusts, unit trusts as investment vehicles, risks posed by trust loss rules, the tax implications of converting a non-fixed trust into a fixed trust, and the consequences of CGT event E4 for unit trusts.

Introduction

Recent years have been a turbulent time for the controllers of trusts and their advisers. While the taxation regime for discretionary trusts has been the focus of much attention, there have also been significant changes for unit trusts, particularly following the 2011 Federal Court decision *Colonial First State Investments Ltd v FCT (Colonial)*.[1]

As set out in the Australian Taxation Office's (ATO) decision impact statement for Colonial, it now seems that, for taxation purposes, very few traditional unit trusts will satisfy the strict definition of a 'fixed trust'.

The former government's discussion paper, A more workable approach for fixed trusts,[2] released following the Colonial decision, succinctly summarises the current uncertainty about the meaning of a fixed trust for taxation purposes and in turn the impact on taxpayers:

> 'In practice, very few trusts will qualify as a fixed trust unless the Commissioner of Taxation exercises the limited discretion to treat a trust as a fixed trust. This creates uncertainty and complexity for taxpayers and means that taxpayers and the Australian Taxation Office incur compliance and administrative costs in preparing and responding to applications to treat a trust as a fixed trust.'

This article considers the specific requirements for a trust qualifying as a fixed trust and the relevance of the fixed trust concept for taxation purposes.

Generally speaking, there are two types of fixed trusts, being 'ordinary fixed trusts' and 'widely held unit trusts'. An ordinary fixed trust is a general term used to describe all trusts which are not 'widely held unit trusts'. As set out above, this article will focus on the rules relating to ordinary fixed trusts and will not consider widely held unit trusts.

For completeness, the following topics, among others, are all potentially relevant in the context of fixed trusts (however, detailed consideration of them is outside the scope of this article):

(1) stamp duty;
(2) land tax;
(3) small business concessions;
(4) Div 7A;
(5) tax consolidations;
(6) the value shifting provisions;
(7) the closely held trust rules; and
(8) corporate unit trusts and widely held public trusts.

What is a fixed trust?

As set out above, the definition of a fixed trust for taxation purposes is currently under review by the government following Colonial, which concluded that the meaning of a fixed trust is narrower than commonly thought by taxpayers and their advisers.

The Colonial case

The decision in the Colonial case has created widespread uncertainty about the meaning of 'fixed trust' for taxation purposes.

Colonial First State Investments Ltd (Colonial First State) was the responsible entity for a retail managed fund, which invested in the units of a wholesale fund, also run by Colonial First State. It proposed to amend the terms of the constitution (i.e. trust deed) of the wholesale fund to give the trustee discretion to stream different types of income to certain redeeming unitholders. Colonial First State applied for a private ruling from the Commissioner as to the tax consequences of the proposed amendment.

A key objective of the amendments was to alleviate the perceived unfairness for some unitholders when streaming capital gains out of the fund. In particular, the amendments were intended to enable the streaming of non-discounted capital gains to unitholders who had held their units for less than 12 months, and in turn to ensure that long-term unitholders could receive the capital gains entitled to the general 50% discount.

One of the questions posed by the private ruling was whether the wholesale fund would be a fixed trust for tax purposes if the proposed amendments were made.

The court considered the definition of 'fixed trust' in the *Income Tax Assessment Act 1997 (Cth) (ITAA97)* which states that, at least for trust loss purposes, a fixed trust is a trust where the beneficiaries have fixed entitlements to the income and capital of the trust, and the definition of 'fixed entitlement' in s 272-5, Sch 2F of the Income Tax Assessment Act 1936 (Cth) (ITAA36) which provides that:

> 'If, under a trust instrument, a beneficiary has a vested and indefeasible interest in a share of income of the trust that the trust derives from time to time, or of the capital of the trust, the beneficiary has a fixed entitlement to that share of the income or capital.'

The court confirmed that a trust will be a fixed trust if the beneficiaries have a vested and indefeasible interest in all of the income and capital of the trust fund under the trust instrument. As the legislation does not define 'indefeasible', the court confirmed that its ordinary meaning should be applied, i.e. 'that interest cannot be terminated, invalidated or annulled'.

The court found that the wholesale fund would not be a fixed trust as the unitholders' interests in the income and capital of the trust were defeasible. This was primarily because of the operation of the provisions of the *Corporations Act 2001* (Cth) which allowed the unitholders to modify, replace or repeal the constitution by special resolution.

Ultimately, the court decided that if a unitholder's interest could be reduced or detrimentally affected as a result of a special resolution of unitholders or other actions of the trustee, the unitholder could not have a 'vested and indefeasible interest', as required by Sch 2F ITAA36.

Given that the vast majority of unit trusts have variation provisions analogous to the one in Colonial, it is likely that, based on the decision, very few trusts in fact create a 'vested and indefeasible' interest in a share of the income or capital of the trust estate.

As set out above, the former government released a discussion paper in July 2012 about the meaning of a fixed trust, and submissions on that discussion paper closed in September 2012. No announcement has since been made concerning proposed changes to the definition of fixed trust. Consequently, there is no formal guidance on what is meant by a fixed trust for tax purposes, and there remains significant uncertainty about how the ATO and the courts will apply the definition.

Further, the ATO's decision impact statement for Colonial confirms that the ATO will offer no further guidance on the meaning of a fixed trust while the government is undertaking its review.

This article does not analyse the merits of the various reform options proposed by the government's discussion paper.

Fixed trusts and unit trusts – not necessarily the same

A unit trust is often an attractive investment vehicle for taxpayers, as it can offer many similar benefits to a corporate structure, with the following additional benefits:

(1) access to the general capital gains tax (CGT) 50% discount;
(2) the ability to issue units with different rights to income and capital;
(3) no requirements for formal disclosure to ASIC and other regulatory bodies; and
(4) no requirements for a formal audit. Unit trusts are often viewed as the preferred structure for holding capital appreciating assets where there are unrelated third party investors.

Traditional unit trusts provide that the beneficial interest in the trust property is held in proportion to the units held by each unitholder. In *CPT Custodian Pty Ltd v Commissioner of State Revenue* (CPT Custodian),[3] the High Court confirmed that there is no rigid meaning of a unit trust.

The ATO has confirmed in ID 2010/57 that a trust will be considered a unit trust for the purposes of Div 6C ITAA36 (which relates to the taxation of public trading trusts) where:

(1) beneficiaries are made entitled to a share of a beneficial interest under a trust, such as an interest in either or both of the income and capital; and
(2) the entitlement is measured by reference to a fixed standard of measurement, irrespective of whether the trust deed labels the interests as 'units'.

It also confirms that where the trust deed uses the phrase 'pro-rata' to specify the relative interests of beneficiaries, then in most occasions of this nature, the holder of the beneficial interest will be a unitholder and the trust will be a unit trust.

As set out above, following the Colonial decision, whether a unit trust is a fixed trust for tax purposes is less than certain.

The test for qualifying as a fixed trust turns on whether the beneficiaries have a vested and indefeasible interest in the trust property. This must be ascertained from the terms of the trust deed, and in light of the guidance offered by Colonial, the following factors will be relevant to supporting that a trust is a fixed trust:

(1) the trustee cannot create different rights or different classes of units;
(2) all units on issue must have the same rights to receive income and capital of the trust;
(3) units must be allotted for market value;
(4) all income and capital of the trust must be distributed in proportion to the unitholdings, i.e. there is no discretion held by the trustee;
(5) partly paid units cannot be issued;
(6) the trust deed requires all unitholders to agree on the redemption of units and any redemption must be at market value;
(7) all valuations of the trust fund, and in turn the determination of unit values, must be conducted by a valuer in accordance with 'applicable Australian accounting principles';
(8) the trustee cannot make gifts; and

(9) the unanimous consent of all unitholders is required to vary the trust deed and the variation power should prohibit amendments to any of the above provisions.

A power within the trust deed permitting the trustee to accumulate the income as corpus should not disqualify a trust from being a fixed trust, provided that the beneficiaries have a vested and indefeasible interest to the accumulated amounts.

Section 272-5 ITAA36 further confirms that the mere fact that units are redeemable, or that further units can be issued, does not mean that a unitholder's interest is defeasible, provided the redemption or issue occurs for market value.

As confirmed in Colonial, having a vested and indefeasible interest is critical to the meaning of 'absolute entitlement' for the purposes of the tax legislation.

'Absolute entitlement' is also a term clouded by uncertainty following the issue of TR 2004/D25 in draft in 2004 by the ATO (which remains unfinalised), and subsequent decisions confirming that it may never be possible to create absolute entitlement where the trustee has a right of indemnity from trust assets (e.g. in *Oswal v FCT (Oswal)*,[4] discussed in more detail below).

However, TR 2004/D25 confirms (notwithstanding that it remains in draft form) that the meaning of absolute entitlement is not relevant for a unit trust, on the basis that the CGT provisions in the ITAA97 treat the units in a unit trust as the relevant asset, rather than the unitholders' interest in the underlying trust property.

It is important to understand the distinction between unitholders having a vested and indefeasible interest in the trust, as opposed to a proprietary interest in the underlying assets of the trust.

In CPT Custodian, the High Court stated that, as was later confirmed in Colonial, the nature of the interest of a unitholder will depend on the terms of the relevant trust deed. In particular, it was held that a sole unitholder was not the equivalent owner of the trust assets due to the trustee's right of indemnity. Under the trustee's right of indemnity, it could sell the assets held by the trust to satisfy that right of indemnity and, as such, a sole unitholder did not have a proprietary interest in the underlying assets of the trust.

Diagram 1

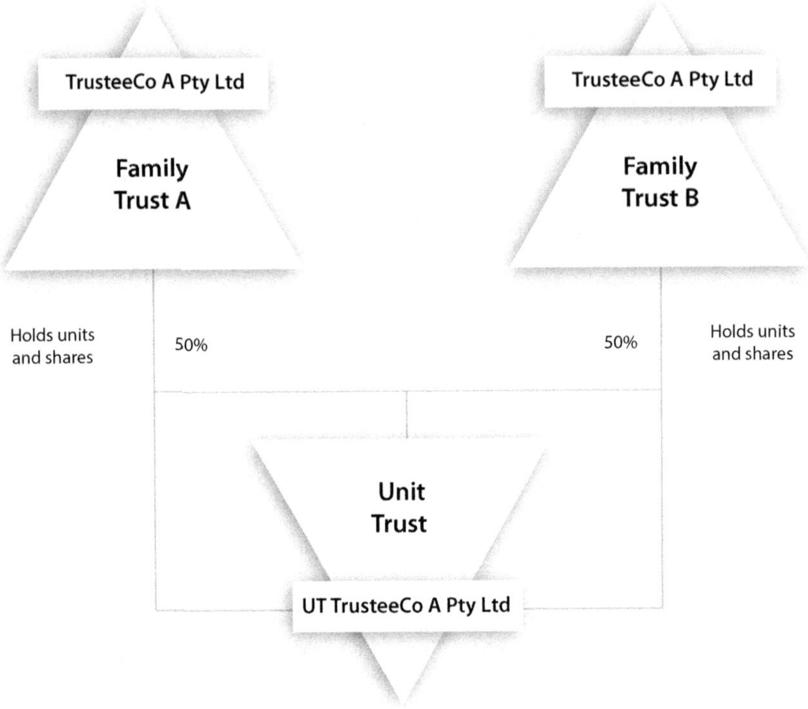

Unit trusts in multi-owner investment structures

UNIT TRUSTS ARE often seen as an ideal vehicle for investment activities between unrelated third parties in capital appreciating assets.

When determining an appropriate structure for a new investment venture, many factors are normally taken into consideration. These include, but are certainly not limited to, issues such as:

(1) protecting the assets;
(2) minimising tax payable on profits, both from an income and capital gains perspective;
(3) flexibility of distributing income;
(4) the ease of adding new investors; and
(5) the ease of an investor's exit.

While a discretionary trust is often the ideal structure for making property investments where only one family group is involved, it is generally not an appropriate vehicle for investments between unrelated third parties.

While a unit trust or company both offer certainty for an investor's interest, given that each investor has a proportionate entitlement to both the income and capital returns of the underlying investment, a unit trust is often the preferred investment structure as it enables access to the general 50% CGT discount.

Common structure

To maximise the combined benefits of discretionary and unit trusts, the investment structure summarised in Diagram 1 is often used for investments between unrelated third parties.

In Diagram 1, the units in the unit trust are owned equally by two passive discretionary trusts. The shareholders of the corporate trustee of the unit trust are the same entities as the unitholders of the unit trust. Each unitholder would likely have a representative director on the board of the unit trust's corporate trustee.

The unitholders will often sign a shareholders' and unitholders' agreement governing the terms of their relationships, in addition to the provisions outlined in the trust deed for the unit trust and the constitution for the corporate trustee.

The unitholders themselves can borrow to finance the acquisition of units in the trust. The borrowed funds are used to subscribe for units in the unit trust, and the unit trust then uses the subscription funds to acquire the underlying assets. Alternatively, the unit trust itself can undertake the borrowings.

Obviously, if the unitholders borrow to subscribe for units, the deductibility of any interest expense on the borrowings is with each unitholder, rather than the unit trust.

Related issues

When establishing a unit trust structure, it is important to ensure the deed is properly crafted to limit liability of the unitholders for debts of the trust. Unlike in a corporate structure, where shareholders are not liable for the debts of the company, there is a general principle that unless specifically excluded by the trust deed, the trustee will have a right of indemnity for the liabilities of the trust against both the trust assets and the unitholders.

Failing to exclude this right of indemnity against the unitholders can therefore significantly undermine the asset protection advantages offered by structuring the investment through a unit trust.

Unitholders can generally access the small business concessions on the disposal of units in a unit trust, provided the usual requirements are met. The 50% general CGT discount should also be available if the units have been held for at least 12 months. It will be important, however, to consider the operation of CGT event E4, discussed in more detail below.

ID 2012/74 considers whether Div 7A ITAA36 applies where unitholders agree to retain their unpaid present entitlements within the trust in order to retire external debt incurred by the unit trust. ID 2012/74 confirms that in the factual scenario considered, because the unitholders agreed to defer receiving their proportionate share of the trust's profits and would continue to benefit in the trust assets proportionately to their unitholding, the unitholders were not providing financial accommodation to the trustee or any other taxpayer. Division 7A would therefore not apply.

The relevance of qualifying as a fixed trust

CLASSIFICATION AS A fixed trust is relevant across a number of areas of the taxation legislation, including:

(1) the ability to pass on franking credits to unitholders;
(2) the ability for a trust to carry forward tax losses;
(3) ease of deductibility of borrowings; and
(4) the application of CGT event E4 to distributions by fixed trusts.

Set out below are specific comments on a number of areas where the classification of a unit trust as a fixed trust is potentially relevant.

Unit trusts and franked dividends

UNLESS A UNIT trust qualifies as a fixed trust, it is generally not a tax effective structure to hold shares in a company that is expected to pay franked dividends. In particular, the ITAA36 imposes strict requirements on when a franked distribution can 'flow through an entity'. An entity which receives a franked distribution can potentially gross up its assessable income for the franking credit and obtain a tax offset equal to the franking credits received.

Division 207 ITAA97 confirms that franking credits cannot flow through a trust to the beneficiaries unless:

(1) the trust is a fixed trust;
(2) the trust is a family trust, i.e. it has made a family trust election; or
(3) the beneficiary receiving the franking credits is a natural person whose tax offset entitlement does not exceed $5,000 for the relevant income year.

Unless a unit trust is a fixed trust, the trust will need to make a family trust election in order to tax effectively stream dividends to beneficiaries.

A trust is only eligible to make a family trust election if it passes the family control test at the end of the specified income year. Family trust elections are made in respect of a family group, and must nominate an individual as the test individual whose family group is to be taken into account in relation to the election.

Once an election is made, it is generally irrevocable, subject to some specific exceptions. If a family trust makes a distribution to someone outside the family group, it will be subject to family trust distribution penalty tax.

Where units in a unit trust are held by unrelated third parties, it will usually be impossible for the unit trust to pass the family control test and therefore it will be prevented from making a family trust election.

Even in circumstances where a unit trust is eligible to make a family trust election, the making of the election can significantly restrict the ability to make tax effective distributions in the future.

Practically, a unit trust will generally need to qualify as a fixed trust in order to enable unitholders to access franking credits.

Status of distributions that are not fixed

Hybrid trusts

A key feature of a unit trust is that distributions are made by the trustee among the unitholders in proportion to the number of units held by each unitholder. A distribution of ordinary income is therefore assessable income to the unitholders. However, a distribution of capital is only taxable in the hands of the unitholder to the extent that it represents assessable income.

A hybrid trust is a general term without certain legal meaning, and is most commonly used to describe a trust where there are both fixed and discretionary entitlements to income and capital of the trust.

As set out above, a critical element of a fixed trust is that the unitholders have a vested and indefeasible interest in the trust property, i.e. that the trustee has no discretion as to each beneficiary's entitlement to income and capital. Therefore, it follows that a hybrid trust will never satisfy the definition of a fixed trust due to the existence of the trustee's discretion.

Where negative gearing is an objective, hybrid trusts have historically been a popular vehicle as they can be structured to give a unitholder fixed rights to income, with a broad range of beneficiaries being entitled to the capital of the trust at the trustee's discretion.

In 2009, the Commissioner released TD 2009/17, which outlined the ATO's view on the deductibility of interest incurred on borrowing funds to acquire an interest in a hybrid trust. In TD 2009/17, the ATO confirms its view that if the trustee has the ability to make discretionary distributions, a deduction for the full amount of interest incurred to fund the acquisition of units in the trust is not available.

In particular, the Commissioner states:

> 'Where the terms of the trust indicate that the borrowed moneys have been used to benefit both the taxpayer and others, an apportionment calculation will be required to determine the taxpayer's interest deduction.'

Decisions following the release of TD 2009/17 indicate that the ability for a taxpayer to deduct their interest expenses for an investment in a hybrid trust will depend heavily on the specific facts and circumstances in each case, particularly with reference to the construction of the trust deed.

Forrest

Following the release of TD 2009/17, the Full Court of the Federal Court considered the principle in *Forrest v FCT*.[5] In that case, Mr Forrest borrowed $4.5m to acquire units in the Minderoo Trust. The Minderoo Trust had both discretionary beneficiaries (Mr Forrest's family members) and Mr Forrest personally as the sole unitholder, and was what would be considered a 'typical' hybrid trust.

The Commissioner argued that due to the discretion held by the trustee in making distributions, there was no certainty that the income of the trust would be distributed to Mr Forrest, and therefore there was not a sufficient nexus between the interest incurred and Mr Forrest gaining or producing assessable income. The Commissioner relied heavily on a provision in the trust deed which allowed the trustee to classify amounts received or disbursed by the trust as income or capital.

Mr Forrest argued that as he was the sole unitholder, he was fully and solely entitled to the ordinary income produced by the Minderoo Trust and could consequently claim a deduction for the full amount of the interest incurred on the $4.5m he borrowed to acquire units in the Minderoo Trust. The operation of the relevant clause, he argued, was a power to classify amounts as being on capital account or income account, and did not affect his entitlement to all of the ordinary income of the Minderoo Trust.

The court concluded that the relevant clause was merely a discretionary power to be used by the trustee in administering the trust and it did not amount to a power to classify a receipt of income incorrectly as a capital gain. Therefore, the full amount of the interest expense incurred was deductible to Mr Forrest.

Somewhat unhelpfully, the court did not consider the Commissioner's view set out in TD 2009/17 that the interest should be apportioned. Consequently, the Commissioner chose not to alter his position outlined in TD 2009/17.

Lambert

In the decision of Lambert and FCT,[6] the Administrative Appeals Tribunal (AAT) denied the taxpayer a deduction for interest incurred on borrowings obtained to fund the purchase of investment properties by a discretionary trust, of which the taxpayer was the trustee. While the documentation indicated that the borrowings were made by the taxpayer in his capacity as trustee of the trust, he argued that the intention was to make the borrowings in his personal name and on-lend the funds under an interest-free loan to the trust.

Although the properties were held by the discretionary trust, the taxpayer in his capacity as trustee signed a deed of variation which purported to ensure that the taxpayer was to receive the entire income from the trust until further notice.

That is, the variation sought to create a fixed entitlement to the income of the trust for the taxpayer.

The arrangement (if successful) would have largely achieved a similar outcome as in Forrest in that the asset would have been owned by a trust, while the taxpayer would have been entitled to a tax deduction on the borrowing expense.

However, the AAT found that the variation was an ineffective exercise of the trustee's power of amendment under the trust deed because it was not executed validly. Also, the amendment was held to be void because it was inconsistent with the trustee's fiduciary duty to vary the deed for the benefit of the beneficiaries as a whole; the attempted amendment was in fact for the sole benefit of the taxpayer.

Furthermore, the AAT rejected that there was sufficient evidence to support an argument that the borrowings were made by the taxpayer in his personal name. Therefore, the interest liability arose to the taxpayer in his capacity as trustee of the trust, and the taxpayer's personal claim for the deductions were denied.

Borrowing by unit trusts

Trustee's power to borrow and mortgage

As with any form of trust, the trustee of a unit trust or fixed trust must consider its fiduciary duty to maintain and protect the assets of the fund when undertaking investments and in particular, when borrowing and offering trust property as security.

While the powers conferred on a trustee vary in each jurisdiction, the trustee has a statutory power to borrow and raise money by granting a mortgage where the trust deed contains a broad power to pay or apply the capital of the trust for any purpose. The trust deed should also contain an express power authorising the trustee to borrow and grant security over the trust property.

'The test for qualifying as a fixed trust turns on whether the beneficiaries have a vested and indefeasible interest in the trust property.'

Investments in unit trusts by self-managed superannuation funds

The meaning of a fixed trust appears frequently within the borrowing and investment framework for superannuation funds in the *Superannuation Industry (Supervision) Act 1993 (Cth)* (SISA).

Borrowing by self-managed superannuation funds is predominantly structured through a form of fixed or bare trust, largely due to the general prohibition in the SISA against superannuation funds borrowing or maintaining a borrowing of money unless the borrowing is a 'limited recourse borrowing arrangement'.

This arrangement allows a trustee of a superannuation fund to borrow money, or maintain a borrowing of money, under an arrangement where, among other requirements, the original asset or replacement asset is effectively held on a bare trust so that the trustee of the superannuation fund acquires a beneficial interest in the asset. In light of this requirement, the bare trust will generally satisfy the definition of a fixed trust.

Given the general restriction on direct borrowing by superannuation funds, a unit trust is often an appropriate vehicle for making investments through superannuation, and is generally structured through:

(1) a jointly held unit trust, provided the unitholders are unrelated;
(2) an ungeared unit trust; or
(3) units acquired in a unit trust before 12 August 1999.

In-house assets

A superannuation fund may invest in a unit trust (subject to the application of the non-arms' length income provisions discussed below) provided that the unit trust is not a related party of the fund.

There is a prohibition in the SISA which restricts the amount of in-house assets that can be owned or invested by a superannuation fund to generally 5% of the market value of the fund's assets.

A unit trust that is controlled by a related party of the fund will be an in-house asset and caught by this prohibition, unless the trust satisfies the exemption in reg 13.22C of the *Superannuation Industry (Supervision) Regulations 1994* (Cth) (i.e. it is an ungeared unit trust).

The test for whether a trust is controlled by a related party of the fund requires consideration of the fixed entitlements of the unitholders. In particular, a related party of the fund will be deemed to control the trust if the fund or its associates have a fixed entitlement to more than 50% of the capital or income of the trust.

There is an exception to the in-house asset test in reg 13.22C for a unit trust that does not have any borrowings, notwithstanding that the trust may be a related party of the superannuation fund. This commonly arises where a superannuation fund wishes to make an investment through a unit trust with other (non-superannuation fund) unitholders who can borrow to invest in the trust, or if no borrowing is required to fund the investment.

To be eligible for the exemption, the following conditions need to be met:

(1) the trust does not borrow;
(2) the trust does not invest in or loan money to individuals or other entities (other than deposits with authorised deposit-taking institutions);
(3) there is no charge over an asset of the trust;
(4) the trust has not acquired an asset from a related party of the fund other than business real property;
(5) the trust has not acquired an asset (apart from business real property) that had been owned by a related party of the fund in the previous three years;
(6) the trust does not directly or indirectly lease assets to related parties other than business real property;
(7) the trust does not conduct a business; and
(8) the trust conducts all transactions on an arm's length basis.

Prior to 12 August 1999, an investment by a superannuation fund in a related unit trust was not an in-house asset. The transitional arrangements following the expansion of the definition of an 'in-house asset' permit a fund to maintain an investment in a pre-12 August 1999 unit trust where the investment was not previously an in-house asset. However, it is relevant to also bear in mind that the sole purpose test and the non-arm's length income provisions may still apply to the investment. Following 30 June 2009, any further investments in a pre-1999 unit trust will be an in-house asset unless a specific exemption applies.

Non-arm's length income

Income derived by a superannuation fund as a beneficiary of a trust, other than because of holding a fixed entitlement to the income, is non-arm's length income of the entity and will be taxed at penalty rates under the non-arm's length income provisions of the ITAA97. It is therefore important to ensure that the unit trust is a fixed trust for taxation purposes if the unitholder is a superannuation fund.

Income derived by a superannuation fund as a beneficiary of a fixed trust will also be non-arm's length income if:

(1) the fund acquired the entitlement under a scheme, or the income was derived under a scheme, the parties to which were not dealing with each other at arms' length; and
(2) the amount of the income is more than the amount that the fund might have been expected to derive if those parties had been dealing at arm's length.

To avoid the impact of the non-arm's length income rules, it is therefore vital for taxpayers and their advisers to ensure that:

(1) no distributions are made to a superannuation fund from a discretionary trust; and
(2) where a superannuation fund owns units in a unit trust, that the unit trust is a fixed trust for tax purposes.

The ATO has expressed the view in TR 2006/7 that the meaning of a 'fixed trust' must be ascertained from the terms of the relevant trust deed.

It is also relevant to note that the non-arms' length income rules may apply where a self-managed superannuation fund allows its fixed entitlement to remain as an unpaid present entitlement, as this does generally not reflect an arms' length arrangement.

When allowing unpaid present trust entitlements in favour of a superannuation fund, it is therefore necessary to ensure that interest on those unpaid distributions is paid by the trust at market rates as would be the case if the superannuation fund and trust were dealing with each other at arm's length.

Are there risks with unit trusts in trust loss rules?

SCHEDULE 2F ITAA36 contains a number of measures intended to restrict recoupment of losses and to prevent the transfer of the tax benefit of losses to an entity that did not bear the economic loss at the time it was originally incurred by the trustee.

As the application of the trust loss rules varies depending on the type of trust in question, the classification of a trust as fixed trust is critical when considering the ability to access trust losses.

Schedule 2F defines 'fixed entitlement' for the purposes of identifying a fixed trust for trust loss purposes. However, as set out above, this definition specifically requires the beneficiaries to have a 'vested and indefeasible' interest in the trust property, the meaning of which is unclear following *Colonial*.

If a trust is considered a fixed trust, it will only need to pass the 50% stake test and income injection test to access the losses within the trust. An excepted trust, which is defined as a fixed trust where all the entitlements to capital and income are held by tax-exempt entities, is entirely exempt from satisfying the trust loss tests.

Table 1 provides a diagrammatic summary of the relevant tests for each type of trust.

50% stake test

The 50% stake test operates to ensure that there has been no significant change in the ownership of a trust. A fixed trust will satisfy the 50% stake test if there are individuals who have fixed entitlements, either directly or indirectly, to more than 50% of the income or capital of the trust estate for the entire relevant period.

If no individual has a stake of more than 50% in the income or capital of the trust for the entire relevant period, the test will not be satisfied.

For example, assuming a trust otherwise satisfies the fixed trust definition, and the following facts apply:

(1) John and Mary have a 70% fixed entitlement to the income and capital of the Smith Family Unit Trust;
(2) Stephen and Jane hold the remaining 30% entitlement;
(3) the Smith Family Unit Trust has a loss in 2010; and
(4) during 2011, John and Mary sell their 70% interest to Nicholas.

In the above example, as the original unitholders owning more than 50% of the fixed entitlements have not held their interest for the entirety of the relevant period, the trust will fail the 50% stake test and the loss cannot be used in the 2011 financial year.

Alternate test for fixed trusts

The 50% stake test will be failed where the units are not held by individuals, for example, in circumstances where the units are held by discretionary trusts.

However, the alternate test for fixed trusts allows the 50% stake test to be passed if non-fixed trusts own more than 50% of the income and capital of the fixed trust, provided those unitholder trusts themselves satisfy the relevant trust loss provisions applying to non-fixed trusts.

Broadly, this means that a unitholder discretionary trust holding more than 50% of the income and capital of a fixed trust must also satisfy both the pattern of distributions test and the control test (summarised below), unless it has made a family trust election.

Table 1		
Fixed trust	Non-fixed trust	Family trust
50% stake test	50% stake test	Modified income injection test
Income injection test	Income injection test	
	Pattern of distributions test	
	Control test	

Income injection test

The income injection test is intended to prevent an 'outsider' of a trust 'injecting' funds into the trust to take advantage of losses.

The income injection test applies where:

(1) the trust has a deduction (including prior year losses) in the income year being examined;

(2) there is a scheme under which the trust derives assessable income, an outsider provides a benefit and a return benefit is provided to the outsider; and

(3) it is reasonable to conclude that the assessable income has been derived or the benefits have been provided, wholly or partly, because the deduction is allowable.

An 'outsider' for the purposes of a fixed trust is any person who is not the trustee of the trust, or a person with a fixed entitlement to a share of the income or capital of the relevant trust.

Deductibility of losses by non-fixed trusts

The trust loss measures applying to a non-fixed trust (i.e. any trust that is not a fixed trust) are significantly more onerous than the measures applying to a fixed trust.

If the trust is a family trust (i.e. a discretionary trust which has made a family trust election), only the income injection test will need to be satisfied. All other non-fixed trusts will have to pass not only the 50% stake test and income injection test (set out above), but also the:

(1) pattern of distributions test; and
(2) control test.

These tests must all be satisfied before a non-fixed trust is able to carry-forward losses.

Pattern of distributions test

The pattern of distributions test considers whether distributions have consistently been made to the same individuals. In practice, this is normally the most difficult test to pass.

A trust passes the pattern of distributions test for an income year if the trust distributed at least 50% of the income and capital to the same individuals, directly or indirectly, in each test year. Although there is no requirement for the individuals who received the income and capital to be the same individuals, if the test is not satisfied for both income and capital, the test is failed.

The test must be satisfied for every year the trust makes distributions out of the preceding six income years. If separate percentages of distributions are made, the smallest distribution percentage during the period is applied to all income years. This is obviously more relevant where the trustee has discretion when determining the distributions from the trust in each income year.

The meaning of 'distribution' is given a wide meaning and includes paying or crediting income or capital (this includes loans), transferring income or capital, reinvesting the income or capital on behalf of a person in accordance with their directions and applying the income or capital to a person's benefit.

Control test

The control test examines whether a different group commences to control the trust after the relevant loss year. A group includes a person and their associates, either alone or together.

A group controls a non-fixed trust if:

(1) the group has the power by means of the exercise of a power of appointment or revocation or otherwise to obtain beneficial enjoyment of the capital or income of the trust;
(2) the group is able, directly or indirectly, to control the application of the capital or income of the trust;
(3) the group is capable, under a scheme, of gaining the beneficial enjoyment referred to in (1) or the control referred to in (2);
(4) the trustee is accustomed, under an obligation or might reasonably be expected to act in accordance with the directions, instructions or wishes of the group;
(5) the group is able to remove or appoint the trustee; or
(6) the group acquires more than a 50% stake in the income or capital of the trust.

The test deals with more practical notions of 'control' rather than changes of trustees within the group. A new trustee or appointor from outside the original group, however, would cause the test to be failed.

Converting a non-fixed trust into a fixed trust – tax implications

IN SOME CIRCUMSTANCES, it may be desirable or commercially necessary to convert a non-fixed or discretionary trust into a fixed trust. However, the CGT consequences of such an exercise need to be examined carefully and in particular, the risk of triggering a trust resettlement (i.e. the creation of a new trust giving rise to CGT event E1).

Resettlement consequences

In 2011, the Full Court of the Federal Court in *FCT v Clark (Clark)*[7] considered the circumstances in which a resettlement would occur. In that case, the trust in question was a unit trust which had been substantially varied over several years by changing the trustee, the beneficiaries and the trust property.

In rejecting the Commissioner's argument that these amendments had amounted to a resettlement of the trust, the court held that the three factors to consider when determining whether there has been a continuum of a trust are:

(1) the terms of the trust deed;
(2) the trust property; and
(3) the membership of the trust.

Further, the court confirmed that where the changes are within the scope of the variation power in the relevant trust deed, changes over time to the trust property and beneficiaries should not trigger a resettlement, provided that they can be identified at all times and there has not been a severance which would lead to the termination of the trust.

Following Clark, the ATO accepted in TD 2012/21 that a valid amendment to a trust not resulting in a termination of the trust will not of itself result in the happening of CGT event E1.

TD 2012/21 confirms that the ATO's position, formerly set out in its statement of principles (SOP), was unsustainable following the court's decision in Clark and that:

'Neither CGT Event E1 nor CGT Event E2 ... happens unless:

a the change causes the existing trust to terminate and a new trust to arise for trust law purposes, or
b the effect of the change ... is such as to lead to a particular asset being subject to a separate charter of rights and obligations such as to give rise to the conclusion that that asset has been settled on terms of a different trust.'

The ATO has also withdrawn the SOP which had set out the ATO's view on when it believed changes to a trust would give rise to a new trust (and therefore trigger CGT consequences).

The ATO has also confirmed in its decision impact statement released for Clark:

> 'To the extent that the High Court in Commercial Nominees left open the possibility that there might be a loss of continuity in circumstances short of the existence of the trust having come to an end, the Commissioner acknowledges that in Clark there were significant changes to the property, membership and operation of the [Trust] without any finding by the courts that there was a loss of continuity such as to deny the trust access to the losses being carried forward.'

Although Clark and the ATO's withdrawal of the SOP have narrowed the ATO's previously wide interpretation of when a variation would amount to a resettlement, there remains some uncertainty about the scope of permissible variations.

The recent decision by the Federal Court in Oswal is one of the first decisions to consider CGT event E1 following Clark.

In this case, the trustee of a discretionary trust resolved to hold shares that were a part of the corpus of the trust on sub-trust for the absolute benefit of certain beneficiaries of the trust.

The trustee, Mr Oswal, argued that the declaration did not create a new trust over the shares, but merely created a separate fund of the relevant assets within the trust. The court agreed with the ATO and held that the resolution by the trustee to make the beneficiaries absolutely entitled to the shares triggered CGT event E1.

This decision would appear to be consistent with one of the examples given by the Commissioner in TD 2012/21. It should be noted, however, that Mr Oswal has appealed the decision to the Full Court of the Federal Court, and the appeal is expected to be heard in December 2013.

Importantly, as Oswal did not expressly discuss Clark or 'resettlements', it offers limited guidance when considering the resettlement consequences of converting a discretionary or non-fixed trust into a fixed trust.

For completeness, Clark confirms the longstanding trust law principle that the variation must be within the scope of the variation power in the relevant trust deed.

Converting a non-fixed unit trust into a fixed trust

In light of the guidance offered by Colonial about the meaning of a fixed trust, it may be appropriate to vary the trust deed for a unit trust to ensure that it qualifies as a fixed trust.

Given the narrow interpretation of the meaning of 'resettlement' following Clark, variations to a trust deed to insert or remove the provisions summarised above should not create any risk of a resettlement, as there would remain continuity of the trust, applying the key indicia of continuity of trust terms, trust property and membership.

Converting a discretionary trust into a fixed trust

The SOP confirmed the ATO's historic view that converting a discretionary trust to a unit trust would trigger a resettlement. However, there is limited guidance following Clark and the withdrawal of the SOP about whether a discretionary trust being converted to a fixed trust, i.e. bestowing a fixed entitlement to income and capital on particular beneficiaries, would amount to a resettlement.

A variation to convert a discretionary trust into a unit trust would result in a material change to the range and entitlements of beneficiaries. However, it is unclear whether this change would be significant enough to trigger a resettlement, particularly in circumstances where the default beneficiaries remain unchanged (which may be a requirement for stamp duty purposes in some states if the trust owns dutiable property).

Importantly, the Commissioner acknowledges in TD 2012/21 that:

> '... assuming there is some continuity of property and membership of the trust, an amendment made to the trust that is made in proper exercise of a power of amendment contained under the deed will not have the result of terminating the trust, irrespective of the extent of the amendments so made so long as the amendments are properly supported by the power.' (emphasis added)

The Commissioner's use of the words 'some continuity' above suggest that, even where there is not absolute continuity of trust property and membership, the Commissioner is willing to accept that significant amendments will not cause the termination of the trust, provided the amendment is made pursuant to a sufficient power of variation.

In cases where there are changes to the beneficiaries of the trust but continuity of the trust property, there should generally be sufficient continuity of the trust, i.e. 'some continuity' in the Commissioner's words. It is therefore arguable that the variations required to convert a discretionary trust to a fixed trust are not so significant as to indicate the continuity of the trust has not been maintained.

It is also relevant to consider the application of CGT events E3 and E5. CGT event E3 happens if a trust over a CGT asset is converted to a unit trust, and just before the conversion, a beneficiary of the trust was absolutely entitled to the asset. CGT event E5 happens if a beneficiary becomes absolutely entitled to a CGT asset of a trust (except a unit trust or a trust to which Div 128 ITAA97 applies) as against the trustee (disregarding any legal disability the beneficiary is under).

If no beneficiary has absolute entitlement, CGT events E3 and E5 will not happen. Although a discussion about the meaning of absolute entitlement is outside the scope of this article, as set out above, the concept of absolute entitlement is largely unsettled, and following the recent Oswal decision, it may in fact be somewhat difficult to establish that CGT event E3 or E5 has been triggered.

Tax issues for unit trusts and CGT event E4

WHILE A UNIT trust is akin to a company in some respects, as the unitholders will have set entitlements to income and capital, a unit trust is a 'flow-through' vehicle for tax purposes, meaning income and capital gains must be distributed to the beneficiaries in proportion to their unitholding, and any undistributed income in each financial year will be taxed at the highest marginal rate.

The consequences of CGT event E4 must be considered when distributing non-assessable income from a unit trust that is a fixed trust for tax purposes. CGT event E4 is relatively complex in practice, and broadly happens if:

(1) the trustee of a trust makes a payment to a taxpayer in respect of the unit or interest in the trust (except for CGT event A1, C2, E1, E2, E6 or E7 happening in relation to it); and
(2) some or all of the payment (the non-assessable part) is not included in the taxpayer's assessable income.

If the trust does not qualify as a fixed trust, CGT event E4 will not apply. The application of CGT event E4 is therefore a relevant consideration when determining whether to establish a unit trust as a fixed or non-fixed trust.

When does CGT event E4 apply?

It is relatively common for non-assessable amounts to be included in a distribution, giving rise to a difference in 'tax law income' and 'trust law income'. That is, the net income of the trust (calculated in accordance with s 95 ITAA36) exceeds the income of the trust available for distribution (calculated in accordance with the deed). This difference could arise for several reasons, including:

(1) expenses chargeable against trust income for that income year but not deductible in that income year;
(2) the small business 50% reduction; or
(3) building allowances in accordance with Div 43 ITAA97.

Ultimately, the objective of CGT event E4 is to increase the tax payable by a unitholder in situations where non-assessable amounts would not otherwise be included in the unitholder's assessable income.

After amendments to the law in 2001, CGT event E4 no longer applies to a payment of the non-assessable general 50% CGT discount. Again, the rules in this regard are relatively complex. However, there are a number of concessionally treated amounts which are excluded when calculating the non-assessable component to ensure that CGT event E4 does not capture concessions which should otherwise be exempt.

There are calls for further reform requesting that timing differences be removed from the scope of CGT event E4, following the release of ID 2012/63, which confirms that CGT event E4 will apply where the trust income exceeds net income for the particular year.

If CGT event E4 is triggered, the cost base of the units is reduced by the non-assessable amount (but not below nil). The taxpayer will make a capital gain if the non-assessable part of the distribution is more than their cost base. However, it is possible to apply the general 50% CGT discount to any capital gain, provided that the taxpayer is not a company and has held its units for longer than 12 months.

Conclusion

Although the benefits of a trust being considered a fixed trust for tax purposes are clear, the definition of a 'fixed trust' is anything but.

While Colonial provides some guidance about the requirements for a unit trust to qualify as a fixed trust, the government's proposed reform of the fixed trust definition and the ATO's response to the Colonial decision create significant uncertainty and complexity for taxpayers and their advisers. For some taxpayers, the lack of flexibility arising from seeking to satisfy the fixed trust criteria suggested by Colonial may in fact outweigh the taxation benefits of qualifying as a fixed trust.

Matthew Burgess, CTA

Disclaimer

This article covers legal and technical issues in a general way. It is not designed to express opinions on specific cases. This article is intended for information purposes only and should not be regarded as legal advice. Further advice should be obtained before taking action on any issue.

References

[1] [2011] FCA 16.

[2] Commonwealth of Australia, A more workable approach for fixed trusts, discussion paper, July 2012.

[3] [2005] HCA 53.

[4] [2013] FCA 745.

[5] [2010] FCAFC 6.

[6] [2013] AATA 442.

[7] [2011] FCAFC 5.

TESTAMENTARY TRUSTS: BESPOKE PLANNING OPPORTUNITIES

Testamentary trusts: bespoke planning opportunities

Abstract

In recent years, the need for effective structuring of business and personal assets has been brought into sharp focus for high net worth individuals and business owners. Fundamental changes to the taxation regime, the vast amounts of wealth accumulated within superannuation funds and the increasing tendency for both business and personal relationships to be relatively short term, as opposed to life long, have meant that traditional estate planning has been revolutionised. This article focuses on the creative use of testamentary trusts in the context of estate planning. The article considers assets that do not form part of an estate, testamentary trusts, tax treatment of testamentary trusts, the attitude of the Australian Taxation Office towards testamentary trusts, trust cloning, trust splitting, bespoke company constitutions and fettering of a trustee's discretion, and changing of domicile.

Introduction

In recent years, the need for effective structuring of business and personal assets has been brought into sharp focus for high net worth individuals and business owners. Fundamental changes to the taxation regime, the vast amounts of wealth accumulated within superannuation funds and the increasing tendency for both business and personal relationships to be relatively short term, as opposed to life long, have meant that traditional estate planning has been revolutionised.

A significant factor to note in the changing face of estate planning is the transfer of wealth from Australia's "baby boomer" generation.

Statistically, this segment of the population is by far the wealthiest and best educated in Australia's history, and consequently far more sophisticated estate planning strategies are being developed in order to minimise the ability for wealth to be attacked by creditors, former spouses, business associates and (in some instances) disgruntled beneficiaries.

While tax effective strategies incorporating complex will arrangements and testamentary trusts continue to be of relevance, recent developments in estate planning have been more focused on the protection of underlying wealth. In particular, additional structures are now being utilised in conjunction with wills to ensure wealth passes efficiently to the intended recipients and that the transfer takes place at the intended time. Often the desire to ensure a suitable tax outcome needs to be balanced against a desire to ensure assets are protected from family disputes, spendthrift beneficiaries and creditors in deciding on an estate plan.

Asset protection strategies and the use of special purpose trusts are important issues to consider in estate planning, particularly where potential beneficiaries are in occupations, professional practice or in business, or where there is a risk that a personal relationship of a beneficiary may degenerate in the future. Potential beneficiaries that fall into any of these "at risk" categories will be exposed to losing assets unless appropriate structures are put in place.

The difficulty in many estate planning exercises is that serious attempts to devise and implement a plan are often not made until some "triggering event" stimulates action. Often the triggering event is itself an issue that may jeopardise the ability to implement appropriate strategies, for example financial or matrimonial misfortune or life-threatening illness.

Given that the first wave of the baby boomer generation is now nearing 60, it is likely that the increased importance placed in recent years on appropriately structuring intergenerational wealth transfers will continue to intensify.

There are an enormous number of aspects to a comprehensive estate plan. This article will focus on the creative use of testamentary trusts in the context of estate planning. In particular, the article will consider the following:

a. assets that do not form part of an estate;
b. testamentary trusts – a refresher;
c. tax treatment of testamentary trusts;
d. the attitude of the Australian Taxation Office (ATO) towards testamentary trusts;
e. trust cloning;
f. trust splitting;
g. bespoke company constitutions and fettering of a trustee's discretion; and
h. changing of domicile.

Each of the above issues is dealt with in turn below.

Assets which do not form part of the estate

PERHAPS ONE OF the most important aspects of modern estate planning is in relation to those assets which do not in fact pass pursuant to a person's will. It is vital in any estate plan for both the client and their advisers, from as early as possible in the estate planning process, to clearly understand which assets are regulated by the person's will and which assets will need to be regulated utilising other strategies.

A brief summary of the main types of assets that do not pass pursuant to a person's will are set out below.

Asset type	Control	Documents regulating
Joint tenancy (as opposed to tenants in common)	Survivor	Position at law
Superannuation (binding nomination)	Member within three years of death	Valid binding nomination
Superannuation (no binding nomination)	Fund trustee post death	Trust deed or terms of pension
Discretionary trust (individual trustee)	Appointor/principal, or in the absence of both, surviving trustee. If no surviving trustee, then legal personal representative of estate	Trust deed or trusts Act

Asset type	Control	Documents regulating
Discretionary trustee (corporate trustee)	Appointor/principal, or in the absence of both, remaining directors of corporate trustee, subject to the shareholder's power to remove	Trust deed or constitution for corporate trustee
Unit trust	As above for discretionary trusts	Ultimate benefit in trust regulated by trust deed and unitholdings
Private company	Director subject to appointment by shareholders	Constitution or shareholders agreement. Transfer of shares may be pursuant to will depending on other documentation
Loan to company or trust	Lender or legal personal representative of lender	Loan agreement may override will
Business interests	Remaining business owners/trustee of will	Business succession agreement/ partnership Act
Life insurance	Policy owner or nominated beneficiary	Insurance policy

The above table is not intended to be an exhaustive list of assets that fall outside a person's will, but rather is used to highlight the importance for clients to work with all their advisers including their financial planner, lawyer, accountant and insurance broker in devising a comprehensive estate plan.

There are an increasing number of examples where a failure to establish legal ownership and the structure of a testators affairs prior to advising them in regard to the distribution and preservation of assets upon death has meant that a testator's objectives are not met. Similarly, there seems to be an increasing number of disgruntled beneficiaries who readily seek to apportion blame where unintended consequences arise.

The various intricacies involved in relation to assets that fall outside a person's estate could be the subject of an entire article in themselves. For the purposes of this article, it is noted simply that the appropriate starting point for any estate plan should be a thorough analysis of those assets which will in fact pass pursuant to a person's will and, in turn, implementing steps to deal with those assets which will not pass pursuant to the will.

Testamentary trusts – a refresher

Overview

TESTAMENTARY TRUSTS ARE simply trusts established pursuant to a will. In recent years, numerous different types of testamentary trusts have included fixed, unit, discretionary (family), hybrid, resulting (constructive), bare, lineal descendent and superannuation proceeds trusts. The various types of trusts have a number of different features and specific uses, but fundamentally the legal structure of all testamentary trusts is very similar.

Structure of testamentary trusts

Essentially, the share of the estate intended for each beneficiary can be managed via a testamentary trust by the trustee appointed by the testator in their will (often the trustee and a beneficiary of the trust may be the same person although the advantages and disadvantages of this approach are dealt with in more detail below).

During each year, the trustees of the trust may have complete discretionary power to choose which beneficiary takes what share of income for that year. They may also have the absolute discretion as to the distribution of capital, but often the distribution of capital can be limited to set amounts and for a limited range of direct descendants, or otherwise as instructed by a testator.

A will maker (or testator) sets out the terms of the trust in their will and can give the trustee complete discretion as to who should receive capital and income from the trust, or alternatively the testator can restrict the trustee's discretion as much as they like.

A "lineal descendant" trust is simply a specific type of testamentary trust whereby the testator may restrict the ability of the trustee so that they may only distribute income or capital (or both) to the testator's children and grandchildren and so on, excluding any spouse of the children and/or grandchildren. The main attraction to excluding spouses as potential beneficiaries is that in the event of a matrimonial (or de facto) relationship breakdown, it is unlikely that a lineal descendant trust would be taken into account by the Family Court as anything other than a resource of the relevant marriage. Thus, the assets of the testamentary trust are likely to be protected in such a scenario.

Conversely, many people argue that the flexibilities normally associated with a trust structure are significantly diminished if a whole class of potential beneficiaries are excluded. In recent times, many people have adopted a "hybrid" approach to testamentary trusts so that spouses can be potential income beneficiaries from year-to-year but that in relation to any capital distributions from the trust, these distributions may only be made to lineal descendants of the original will maker.

Advantages of testamentary trusts

The main advantages of an appropriately drafted testamentary discretionary trust (TDT) established by a will are as follows:

a the flexibility given to the trustees to allocate income and capital with reference to the facts at the time, rather than a testator's prediction (no matter how careful) of the future. It allows the trustee to make a greater distribution for a testator's child with a special need, such as (in particular) wastrel children, as well as those with a disability;

b if an estate was left to a child absolutely, then it is their property and could be jeopardised by their financial position at the time of death or after. In addition, should that child suffer matrimonial or financial misfortune at some time in the future, the trust at least provides a facility whereby the inheritance can be kept separate. As indicated above, it is unlikely (particularly where spouses are not potential beneficiaries) that the assets of the

TDT would be seen as anything more than a resource for the relevant beneficiary and not part of the assets of the matrimonial pool which are physically distributed between the parties to the marriage breakdown;

c the TDT can be drafted such that it complies with the requirements set out in s 102AG(2)(a)(i) of the Income Tax Assessment Act 1936 (Cth) (ITAA36) so that income each year allocated to minor children is not subject to the same tax rates as if it were a normal family discretionary trust established during a person's lifetime (where the first $7416 distributed to a child is tax free but then any further income is taxed at the highest rate which could be up to 66%);

d where income is derived under the section quoted above, infant children are assessed at the normal, individual rates (approximately $24,000 tax free and the balance at normal adult rates) which may be a significant saving in tax when you look at the gross income for a family unit. The Commissioner does have some discretion in these cases, but generally the discretion is exercised in favour of the TDTs as they are a "traditional" form of trust; and

e even if, for any reason, the trust does not come into effect through the operation of law, or it fails, then the will can include a fall-back provision whereby the capital vests in the intended beneficiary anyway, with provision for their children if necessary, or even revert to trusts established for other beneficiaries.

Ultimately TDTs are particularly useful structures in the following circumstances:

a to ensure concessional tax treatment is available to distributions of capital and income to minor beneficiaries;

b to protect accumulated wealth from wastrel or spendthrift beneficiaries;

c to provide for infant children and disabled beneficiaries; and d to protect inheritances from attack by the family law courts and trustee in bankruptcy.

Disadvantages of testamentary trusts

There are a number of potential disadvantages to TDTs, including:

a once income is determined to be distributed to an infant and is then not applied in payment of the infant's needs, there will be an accumulating debt owing to that infant by the TDT. Thus, when the time comes to wind up the trust and for the beneficiaries to take the capital, they may find the capital substantially eroded by the necessity to pay these debts to the children or other beneficiaries, unless of course they are in some way forgiven. Alternatively, when the relevant child reaches the age of majority, it may be that they seek repayment of the loan owed to them;

b the TDT structure requires a reasonable degree of control, similar to a normal family discretionary trust, including recourse to competent accountants and lawyers for trust administration advice. This all involves a cost;

c the taxation aspects of a TDT have not been ably and forcefully contested in a court in recent years. Notwithstanding this, the language of s 102AG(2)(a)(i) is clear and there are income tax rulings (both private and public rulings) given in favour of the establishment of TDTs; and

d where the beneficiary of a trust is also a trustee, they should for safety's sake always have at least one trustee with them when undertaking trust-related issues, so the beneficiary will need to be able to work with their co-trustee/s. Protection against creditors or former spouses is diminished when a beneficiary is the sole trustee of the trust, as that beneficiary has power as trustee to distribute the whole of the income and/or capital to themselves. Finding suitable cotrustees can be a difficult exercise, and can also cause increased expenses where a professional is appointed.

e Tax treatment of testamentary trusts

Is Div 6AA limited to income derived from estate assets?

Section 102AG(2)(a)(i) and (2)(d)(i) of Div 6AA ITAA36 make it clear that the provisions are not limited to income derived from estate assets. Under s 102AG(2)(a)(i), excepted trust income is the amount which is assessable income of a trust estate that resulted from a will, codicil or court order varying a will or codicil. Importantly, the subsection only prescribes how the trust estate is deemed to have arisen and does not place any limitations on the management of the trust estate, or on the assets which the trust may hold.

The fact that estate assets forming part of the trust estate may be realised and others may be acquired has no implications on the validity of a testamentary trust, nor the ability of the trustee of a testamentary trust to treat the income as excepted. Similarly, if the trustee decides to borrow money and acquire assets which earn income, then Div 6AA applies to that income.

What limitations might be imposed

Section 102AG(3) contains an exception for non-arm's length arrangements. In particular, it provides that if any two or more parties to:

a the derivation of the excepted trust income mentioned in s 102AG(2); or
b any act or transaction directly or indirectly connected with the derivation of that excepted trust income,

were not dealing with each other at arm's length in relation to the derivation of income, or in relation to the act or transaction, the excepted trust income is only so much (if any) of that income as would have been derived if they had been dealing with each other at arm's length in relation to the derivation, or in relation to the act or transaction.

Essentially, this means that if, say, the loan was not at arm's length, but at a more favourable interest rate compared with the market, then the income derived would have been less, and therefore the amount which can be treated as excepted trust income is reduced.

The case of *The Trustee for the Estate of the Late AW Furse No. 5 Will Trust v FCT*[1] is one of the few reported decisions dealing with Div 6AA. In this case, a will made in July 1974 established multiple testamentary trusts, each for a capital of $1 after the testator passed away shortly after making the will. A trustee was then appointed over one of the testamentary trusts and proceeded to borrow small amounts of money and acquire a unit in a unit trust. The ATO did not consider the income from the unit as excepted income and argued that the income derived by the trustee was not assessable income of a trust estate that "resulted from a will".

Justice Hill rejected the ATO's argument and held that it was only necessary that the parties be dealing on an arm's length basis and that it was not necessary that they be arm's length parties. The court noted that provided the trust estate was created by a will and the arm's length test applied, then any income of a testamentary trust would be considered as excepted trust income.

A secondary issue that was not explored by the ATO was the potential for a Pt IVA ITAA36 argument given the circumstances where the testator created a will shortly before his death establishing a number of testamentary trusts with nominal capital. That said, testators and trustees must, therefore, take care when establishing testamentary trusts under a will to ensure that the arrangement does not fall within the anti-avoidance provisions.

In addition, income from distributions by trusts established prior to death will not enjoy excepted trust income status because the parties are not dealing at arm's length, unless the trustee gives arm's length consideration for the payment.

Testamentary trust distributions to infant beneficiary via inter vivos trust

Where there is a distribution of income from a testamentary trust to an inter vivos trust and then to an infant beneficiary, the better view appears to be that the distribution does not have the status of excepted trust income.

Section 102AG(1) requires that a trust have a prescribed person (essentially an infant, subject to certain exceptions in s 102AC(2) ITAA36) as a beneficiary. Although it could be argued that a testamentary trust has, as its ultimate beneficiary, an infant, and although s 102AG(1) does not expressly exclude an indirect interest as a beneficiary, s 102AG(1) is likely to be construed as dealing only with direct beneficiaries of a testamentary trust.

Having said this, there is an argument that the income of the "trust estate" contemplated in the opening words to s 102AG(2) need not be the same trust estate, and that the income received by an infant beneficiary via an existing family trust is excepted trust income "in relation to a beneficiary of the trust estate (that is the family trust) to the extent to which the amount – (a) is assessable income of a trust estate (that is the testamentary trust) that resulted from – (i) a will".

Distributions following Bamford

One of the critical outcomes of the High Court's decision in *Bamford*[2] *is* the determination of the meaning of the term "income" under s 97 ITAA36. As has been well documented, the High Court concluded that in determining the "income of the trust estate" for the purposes of s 97, consideration needs to be given to the deed, rather than the ordinary concept of income. In the context of a testamentary trust, the deed obviously is the terms set out under the will. Support for this position was garnered from, among other sources, the distinct wording incorporated within s 97 between "income of the trust estate" and "net income of the trust estate".

Practically, therefore, all testamentary trust wills must incorporate powers for a trustee to determine what is and what is not included as income for the trust. Among other things, this should include the ability for the trustee to determine whether or not to include net or gross capital gains as trust income. While this should be possible for newly crafted testamentary trust wills, for any testamentary trusts established under deceased estates careful reviews should be undertaken.

The other main component of the decision in *Bamford* related to the appointment of trust distributions to beneficiaries. The High Court considered the meaning of the term "share" for the purposes of s 97.

A "percentage" approach simply assigns a set proportion or percentage of the income to individual beneficiaries. In contrast, a "fixed amount" approach involves the trustee resolving to appoint a fixed amount of income to an individual beneficiary. Thus, fixing the amount of the distribution of income for say, two of three beneficiaries of the trust with the remaining being distributed to the third beneficiary means that any increase or decrease in assessable income would only affect the distribution to the third beneficiary.

The High Court in *Bamford* held that "share" in the context of s 97 referred to the proportionate entitlement of each beneficiary to the income of the trust estate. Thus, it is the proportion that determines the amount of assessable income that is attributed to the beneficiary, even if fixed amounts have been appointed to the beneficiaries under the trust.

Assuming that trustee resolutions (or minutes) are appropriately crafted in the context of the High Court's decision in *Bamford*, there should not be any particular concern for distributions out of testamentary trusts as a result of this aspect of the *Bamford* decision.

Having said this, in relation to a testamentary trust where the income and capital beneficiaries are different (a classic example in this regard would be a "lineal descendant" testamentary trust where the income beneficiaries are crafted far more widely than the capital beneficiaries), there is potential for significant adverse consequences to arise.

Furthermore, in situations where a testamentary trust already exists because the relevant will maker has died, the relevant parties involved will need to be very careful to ensure in fact that they hold the requisite powers as, speaking generally, it is often not possible to amend the trust instrument following the death of the will maker.

Main residences

Generally, a main residence will be either exempt or fully exempt from capital gains tax (CGT) on its disposal. This position is effectively maintained where a property was the main residence of a deceased immediately prior to their death.

The two key rules are:

a if a property was exempt under the main residence exemption before the death of the deceased owner, and a beneficiary moves into the dwelling and it becomes that beneficiary's main residence, the main residence exemption will continue to be fully available; and

b if a beneficiary sells the dwelling within 24 months of the date of death of the deceased person whose main residence the dwelling was, whether or not that beneficiary resides in the property, the property will be exempt from CGT (under what is known as "the 24-month rule").

Where assets are held as joint tenants, the surviving joint tenant is treated as if the dwelling had passed to the surviving owner "as a beneficiary in a deceased estate".[3] The calculation of the 24-month period will be from the date of death until settlement of the disposal, rather than exchange of contracts.

It should be noted that under s 118-195 of the *Income Tax Assessment Act 1997* (Cth) (ITAA97), it does not matter that the dwelling was not the deceased's main residence, or it was used for income-producing purposes, for a period of time during their ownership. The only requirement is that the dwelling was the deceased's main residence just before their death and was not being used for income-producing purposes at that time.

Main residence exemption and testamentary trusts

As outlined above, the CGT main residence exemption in s 118-195 will apply to capital gains made in relation to dwellings owned by individuals whose interest in the dwelling was passed to them as "a beneficiary in a deceased estate, or as trustee of a deceased estate". A "trustee of a deceased estate" would include only the legal personal representative (LPR) and not a testamentary trust trustee.

Unfortunately, there is no statement from the ATO similar to that in PS LA 2003/12 (discussed below) which confirms that a testamentary trust trustee will be treated the same way as an LPR for the purposes of Div 118 ITAA97. Therefore, the only certain way for the main residence exemption under s 118-195 to apply will be to either to ensure that:

a the property is disposed of by either the LPR or an individual beneficiary (ie without passing to a testamentary trust) within 24 months of the date of death of the deceased; or
b the deceased's main residence does not pass to a testamentary trust with the remainder of the estate assets and is instead passed directly to an individual beneficiary as owner, and to have the deceased's spouse or a person with a right to occupy the house as their main residence.
c However, it would be open to argument that, if a deceased's main residence passed to an individual testamentary trust trustee who then held that property on trust solely for the benefit of either:
d the deceased's spouse; or
e a person with a right to occupy the house under the deceased's will,

and those persons did occupy the dwelling as their main residence, the exemption would remain available to the testamentary trust trustee on a subsequent disposal of the dwelling.

In practice, it is often the case that multiple testamentary trusts are established where a main residence is involved. One (or more) testamentary trust would be established to hold the residuary estate and those testamentary trusts would generally have a wide range of beneficiaries.

An additional testamentary trust would then also be established to hold only the main residence of the deceased. The beneficiaries of the testamentary trust would be limited to:

a the deceased's spouse; or
b a person with a right to occupy the house under the deceased's will.

It is vital that if a person other than the deceased's spouse is to live in the dwelling, that that person is given the right to occupy the house under the terms of the will.

Main residence – partial exemptions

The general rules regarding absences from a main residence are set out in s 118-45 ITAA97 and apply in deceased estate cases equally as in the case of disposals during a person's lifetime.

The general rule for post-CGT dwellings is that the exemption is pro-rated by reference to the number of days that were non-main resident days of both the deceased and the beneficiary (or LPR) over the total ownership period of the dwelling by the deceased and the beneficiary.[4]

Section 118-200 ITAA97 sets out a partial exemption for a beneficiary or LPR where the full main residence exemption under s 118-195 is unable to be accessed. The partial exemption will generally apply in situations where:

a a beneficiary did not occupy the dwelling for their entire ownership period commencing from the date of death of the deceased where the dwelling was either a pre-CGT asset of the deceased or was the deceased's main residence immediately prior to their death; or

b although the dwelling has been the beneficiary's main residence for the entire period of time since the death of the deceased, it was not the main residence of the deceased just before the deceased's death.

Where a dwelling or family home has been used for income-producing purposes by either the deceased or a beneficiary or LPR, a partial exemption may apply where the income-producing activity does not constitute the entire usage of the dwelling. These exemptions are set out in ss 118-190 and 118-92 ITAA97 and will not be discussed in further detail in this article.

ATO attitude to testamentary trusts

Transfer of assets

On the death of a will maker, each asset of the estate will potentially be transferred three times:

a from the will maker to the LPR;
b from the LPR to the beneficiary of the estate, which may be the trustee of a testamentary trust; and
c from the testamentary trust to a beneficiary either as a capital distribution during the lifetime of the trust or as a distribution of corpus upon vesting.

The CGT consequences of each of the abovementioned transfers must be separately considered.

Distributions from will maker to LPR

The first roll-over to examine is the initial transfer of a deceased's assets from the deceased person to their LPR for distribution under the terms of the deceased's will. As a starting point, the general position is that, when a taxpayer dies, any capital gain or loss from any event relating to a CGT asset owned by the deceased is disregarded under s 128-10 ITAA97. This means that the distribution from the deceased to their LPR does not result in a CGT liability for the deceased and there are effectively no other CGT consequences for the deceased.

As to the consequences to the LPR, the CGT assets are taken, under s 128-15 ITAA97 to have been acquired by the LPR on the date the deceased died. The cost base of the CGT asset (other than for a property which was a main residence for the deceased immediately before they died, which is discussed below) for the LPR is modified under s 128-15(4) so that:

a for pre-CGT assets in the hands of the deceased — the first element of the LPR's cost base (and reduced cost base) is the market value of the asset on the day the deceased died (meaning that pre-CGT assets in the hands of the deceased become post-CGT assets in the hands of the LPR); and
b for post-CGT assets in the hands of the deceased — the first element of the LPR's cost base (and reduced cost base) is the deceased's costs base (or reduced costs base) at the date of their death (ie the deceased effectively passes their cost base and reduced cost base to the LPR).

Distributions from LPR to testamentary trust

From a CGT perspective, a testamentary trust is treated much the same as other trusts. However, it should be noted that CGT event E1[5] does not apply to a testamentary trust since that event only applies to the creation of a trust "by declaration or settlement". In the testamentary trust scenario, there is no such declaration of trust and there is no initial settlement sum.

The CGT rules which apply to the distribution from the deceased to the LPR apply equally to subsequent distributions from the LPR to a "beneficiary". It would appear that "beneficiary" for the purposes of the ITAA97 includes the trustee of a testamentary trust (however, you will see later in this article that, for the purpose of Div 128 ITAA97, the trustee of a testamentary trust is also treated the same as an LPR by the ATO).

A CGT asset is taken to have passed to a beneficiary of a deceased's estate if the beneficiary (or in this case, the trustee of the testamentary trust) becomes the owner of the asset whether under the terms of:

a the deceased's will;
b under the intestacy laws; or
c under a deed of arrangement.[6]

As with the initial transfer from the deceased to the LPR, on a subsequent distribution from the LPR to a testamentary trust, any capital gain or loss that the LPR (rather than the deceased) makes is disregarded (although this time, the relevant provision is found in s 128-14(3) ITAA97, rather than s 128-10 ITAA97).

Again, the testamentary trust trustee is taken to have acquired the CGT assets of the deceased at the date of the deceased's death (rather than on the date they were distributed by the LPR) and the first element of the cost base (and reduced cost base) for the testamentary trust trustee will be:

d for pre-CGT assets in the hands of the deceased — the market value of the asset on the day the deceased died; and

e for post-CGT assets in the hands of the deceased — the deceased's costs base (or reduced cost base) at the date of their death.[6]

The testamentary trust trustee is also able include in its cost base any expenditure the LPR has incurred, up to the time of the disposal by the LPR, that the LPR would have been entitled to include in its cost base had it retained the asset.[7]

Distributions from testamentary trust

In 2003, the ATO released PS LA 2003/12, which states that its purpose is to inform ATO staff that the Commissioner will not depart from the long-standing administrative practice of treating the trustee of a testamentary trust in the same way as an LPR is treated for the purposes of Div 128 (and in particular s 128-15(3)). This is generally accepted to mean that there is an exemption from CGT covering the "transfer" from the LPR to the trustee of the testamentary trust in the first instance as well as the subsequent transfer to an eventual beneficiary of the estate. This subsequent transfer may either involve a capital distribution being made by the trustee of the trust to a beneficiary during the lifetime of the trust, or a payment of capital upon vesting of the trust.

The result of PS LA 2003/12 is that, on the subsequent disposal of a CGT asset from a testamentary trust trustee to a beneficiary of the testamentary trust:

a any capital gain or loss that the testamentary trust trustee makes is disregarded under s 128-15(3); and
b the beneficiary will be taken to have acquired the CGT assets of the deceased at the date of the deceased's death (rather than on the date they were distributed by the LPR) and the first element of the cost base and reduced cost base for the beneficiary will be:
   (i) for pre-CGT assets in the hands of the deceased — the market value of the asset on the day the deceased died; and
   (ii) for post-CGT assets in the hands of the deceased — the deceased's cost base (or reduced cost base) at the date of their death.[8]

Ultimately, under PS LA 2003/12 s 128 (in particular s 128(2), (3) and (4)) effectively applies twice:

a initially, when the LPR is the "LPR" for the purposes of Div 128 and the testamentary trust trustee is the "beneficiary"; and
b subsequently, when the testamentary trust trustee is treated as an "LPR" for the purposes of Div 128 and the beneficiaries of the testamentary trust are treated as the "beneficiaries".

CGT event K3

The ATO has indicated that the position in PS LA 2003/12 is subject to CGT event K3, which covers assets passing to tax-advantaged entities. CGT event K3 operates to ensure that, where assets pass to concessional taxed entities from a deceased estate, a capital gain or loss is recognised in the deceased's final tax return, preventing assets with embedded capital gains from avoiding capital gains when they are later disposed of by the concessionally taxed entity. CGT event K3 has, in the past, been avoided by ensuring an asset does not pass to a concessionally taxed entity until after the deceased's standard amendment period (generally four years after the assessment) has expired.

As part of the 2011-12 Budget measures, it was announced that amendments would be made to ensure that where CGT event K3 happened outside of the deceased's standard amendment period, a CGT liability still arose in the deceased's tax return. It was proposed this could be achieved by excluding CGT event K3 from the standard amendment period.

In particular, the CGT event would have been deemed to happen to the relevant entity that passed the asset to the concessionally taxed entity (rather than with the beneficiary), avoiding the need to amend the deceased's tax return. This change would have allowed the entity to which CGT event K3 applied to be able to utilise their realised capital losses against CGT event K3, instead of the deceased utilising their capital losses against their capital gain from CGT event K3.

The change would have been consistent with how Div 128 operates under PS LA 2003/12 where an LPR or testamentary trust trustee sells an asset to a third party, rather than passing the asset to the intended beneficiary of the estate.

However, as with other proposed changes mentioned below, the announced changes to CGT event K3 were abandoned in late 2013.

Legislating CGT exemption for testamentary trust distribution of asset

In the 2011-12 and 2012-13 Federal Budgets, it was proposed that the current ATO practice set out in PS LA 2003/12 of allowing a testamentary trust to distribute an asset of a deceased person without a CGT taxing point occurring would be codified. While draft legislation to effect the change was prepared, the 2013 Federal Coalition Government announced that it was reviewing the progress of a large number of unenacted legislative announcements and ultimately confirmed the amendments would not be implemented.

It is assumed that the ATO will continue to adopt the approach set out in PS LA 2003/12. However, there remains a clear risk that the ATO may abandon the approach on the basis that it arguably has no basis at law given that s 128-15 only refers to an LPR, not the trustee of a testamentary trust expressly.[9]

Where an intended beneficiary dies before administration is completed

The Federal Government released a proposal paper "Minor amendments to the capital gains tax law" in June 2012 which specifically addressed the circumstance where the intended beneficiary dies before administration of an estate is completed. Generally, in that situation, s 128-15 provides a CGT roll-over provided that the asset passes from the first deceased's LPR to the beneficiary's LPR.

However, no CGT roll-over exists where the asset passes (ultimately) from the first deceased's LPR via the second deceased's LPR to the trustee of a testamentary trust or a beneficiary of the intended beneficiary's (ie the second deceased) estate because the asset was not one which the intended beneficiary owned when they died.

The Labor Federal Government in power until July 2013 proposed to introduce measures to allow the intended beneficiary's LPR to access the roll-over where the intended beneficiary dies before an asset that the first deceased owned passes to them, regardless of whether it passes first to a testamentary trust trustee. Again, however, the 2013 Federal Coalition Government confirmed the amendments will not be implemented.

Trust cloning and trust splitting

Where assets have been built up in one trust, there is often a desire for the assets to be divided among different trusts. This may be for a number of reasons, including:

a to allow some assets to be controlled by certain family members and other assets to be controlled by different family members;
b to separate passive investments or valuable capital assets from the risks associated with carrying on a business; or
c to separate multiple business activities and quarantine the risks associated with each.

Transactions of this nature can have a number of consequences, including:

a CGT on asset transfer;
b stamp duty; and
c trust resettlement due to variations of the trust deed.

Trust cloning and splitting can offer pathways to achieve a restructure of testamentary trust assets while minimising adverse transaction costs.

Trust cloning is synonymous with trust "mirroring". That is, assets of a trust are transferred to a separate identical trust or trusts, with no changes to the meaning or effect of the trust deed. This provides for different trust estates.

In contrast, trust splitting is where the assets of the trust are split (within the same trust) so that different trustees are appointed for each part. The ability to split a trust will depend largely on whether the trust deed includes a power to appoint a separate trustee in respect of those assets to be separated from the remaining assets.

For both cloning and splitting, care must be taken to identify the location of each asset of the trust for duty purposes, as different states have different requirements for each potential exemption.

Trust cloning

While the heyday of trust cloning ended with the abolition of the CGT "cloning" exemption (other than in relation to certain forms of fixed trusts), trust cloning is still potentially relevant for all forms of trusts, including testamentary trusts. Although in many instances cloning itself may no longer be effective from a tax perspective, it is important to understand its history from a tax perspective and its future from a stamp duty perspective.

Cloning was (and to some extent still is) an effective tool regularly used in succession planning, asset protection and arranging finance. A properly crafted trust clone arrangement can still be effective from a Queensland duty perspective. Cloning may therefore be worth considering if the tax consequences of the transfer can be otherwise managed, for example if:

a. there has not been a significant increase in the market value of the asset since it was purchased;
b. the small business CGT concessions in Div 152 ITAA97 are available; or
c. the assets to be transferred are nonCGT assets which might otherwise be subject to duty and the income tax consequences can be managed.

As discussed in more detail below, trust splitting does not provide the same level of asset protection as trust cloning. As a result, trust cloning may still be appropriate in some circumstances if the CGT consequences of cloning can be otherwise managed.

Trust splitting

The practical uses of trust splitting are broadly the same as those of trust cloning. As there are different mechanisms required for trust splitting, however, the asset protection afforded is not as substantial as that from trust cloning.

As discussed above, trust cloning involves establishing a separate, discrete trust and transferring assets between the two trusts. Trust splitting, on the other hand, involves establishing a "sub-trust" within the original trust, so there is still only one trust, but different trustees are appointed for different assets held within that trust. The splitting of a trust does not involve a change to the beneficiaries or to the powers conferred on the trustee. The ability to split a trust will depend on the powers provided in the trust deed (which for most testamentary trusts is the will) to appoint a separate trustee in respect of those assets which have been split.

The diagram below illustrates the broad structural differences between the two approaches.

Diagram 1

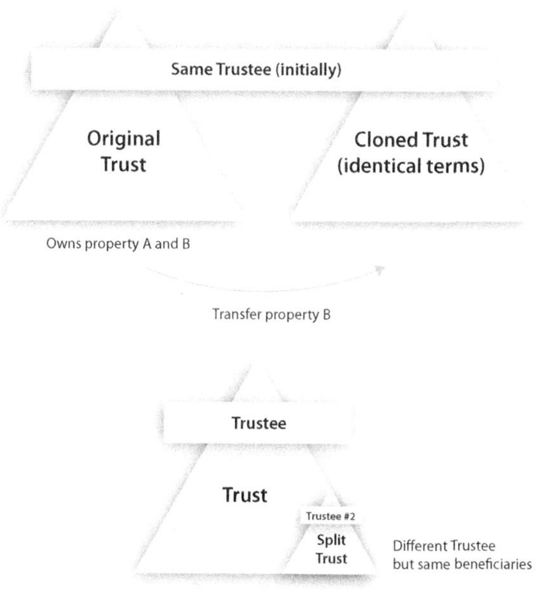

Trust splitting may not be ideal from a succession planning perspective, as there can be practical difficulties in relation to separating the control of the original trust and the subtrust. In particular, as a minimum the following issues would need to be addressed:

a how any principal, appointor or guardian roles are structured under the trust deed;
b the effect of any family trust election (the potential ability to make a oneoff change to a family trust election does not generally assist with trust splitting, as only one family trust election can be made for the trust as a whole); and
c the ability (or inability) to obtain separate tax file numbers and GST registrations for the original trust and the subtrust, if required.

In some cases, where liability and asset protection issues are not important and some ongoing cooperation amongst the trustees of the original trust and the subtrust is feasible, trust splitting can be a useful tool in succession planning.

As the assets are still held in the same trust, albeit with different trustees appointed, this effectively limits the CGT consequences of trust splitting. In particular, while there is a change of legal owner when a new trustee is appointed, the exception under the CGT rules regarding a mere change of trustee should be available.

The more difficult issue in most cases is that the terms of the will must permit splitting (ie allowing separate trust funds) and the power to appoint more than one trustee for those separate funds.

For trusts established outside a will, generally, it should be possible to insert the required powers into an existing trust deed without triggering a resettlement. This issue needs to be considered as part of a careful review of the trust deed and in the context of the ATO's position following the withdrawal of its statement of principles (SOP) on creation of a new trust (further comments in this regard are set out below).

In relation to testamentary trusts, the issues in this regard are more problematic because:

a many testamentary trusts have no variation power; and
b even if there is a variation power, use of it for any purpose may be invalid on public policy grounds (ie as it allows a will maker's directions to be changed after death).

Stamp duty

In relation to the stamp duty consequences of a trust clone or trust split, the rules in each state are different, in some instances depending on the underlying assets that are to be the subject of the rearrangement. It is therefore important to seek specialist advice before embarking on a trust clone or trust split. In broad terms:

a Queensland allows trust cloning of dutiable property without triggering stamp duty;
b it is possible to perform a trust clone in New South Wales in relation to shares in a land rich company (regardless of where that company is registered). There will, however, still be marketable securities duty payable if the company is registered in New South Wales or South Australia; and
c other states allow some form of trust splitting to occur without triggering a stamp duty liability, however, the exact mechanisms vary not only between jurisdictions, but also depending on the underlying assets involved and the terms of the existing trust deed.

Specific comments on the taxation consequences of splitting

As noted above (other than in relation to some forms of fixed trusts), the CGT exemption on trust cloning is no longer available. Generally CGT relief should be available on trust splitting and the basis for this is outlined in more detail below.

CGT events

The CGT events which may have potential application to a trust split are A1, E1 and E2.

CGT event A1 arises on a disposal of an asset. However, where there is a disposal as a result of a new trustee being appointed for particular assets, the exception regarding a mere change of trustee should be available.

CGT event E1 arises if a trust is created over a CGT asset. Splitting does not generally create a new declaration of trust or settlement. A new trust should not arise merely by appointing a new trustee in respect of particular assets held by the trust, and therefore CGT event E1 should not apply.

CGT event E2 occurs where an asset is transferred to a trust. With a trust split, CGT event E2 does not occur as the assets are still held in the same trust, although different trustees are appointed.

In ATO ID 2009/86, it was decided that a trust split did trigger CGT event E1 on the basis that there was a "fundamental change to the rights and obligations attaching to the trust assets". In these particular circumstances, there were a number of factors which gave rise to the ATO's conclusion that a new trust had been created, namely:

a there was a release by the original trustee of its right of indemnity against the assets transferred;
b there was no right of indemnity by the new trustee against the assets which the original trustee retained;
c a separate appointor was nominated for the assets transferred to the split trust; and
d there was a narrowing of the class of beneficiaries who could benefit from the assets transferred to the split trust, by way of a family agreement in which beneficiaries agreed to limit the distributions of the split trust to particular beneficiaries, to the exclusion of others.

In summary, the ATO gave the following reasons for its conclusion that CGT event E1 occurred, namely:

a the trustee's rights were altered by excluding the transferred assets from its right of indemnity; and
b the rights of beneficiaries were altered in that the class of persons who could benefit from the transferred assets had been narrowed.

Resettlement

Trust resettlement is an area that continues to be important for trust splitting, especially where the original trust needs to be varied before the splitting takes place. The consequences of a resettlement include:

a all assets are treated as having been disposed of by the original trust and settled on the new trust (ie CGT event E1 occurs); and
b any losses in the trust are trapped and cannot be carried forward to offset income in the "new" trust.

The ATO in its SOP provided an outline of what it believed may give rise to a resettlement of the trust. The guidance provided by the SOP indicated that a resettlement will arise where there has been an alteration to the trust sufficient to constitute a new trust relationship. The SOP confirmed that a mere change of trustee does not trigger a CGT event. However, the SOP noted that "a change in the trustee or the control of the trustee may be an element in arrangements which in their entirety amount to the creation of a new trust".

The ATO withdrew its SOP following the decision of the Full Court of the Federal Court of *Australia in FCT v Clark (Clark)*[10] in 2011. In that case, the trust in question was a unit trust which had been substantially changed over several years by changing the trustee, the beneficiaries and the trust property. In rejecting the Commissioner's argument that these amendments had amounted to a resettlement of the trust, the court held that the three factors to consider in determining whether there has been a continuum of the trust are:

a the terms of the trust deed (which as noted above, are normally set out in a will for testamentary trusts);
b the trust property; and
c the membership of the trust.

Further, the court confirmed that where the changes are within the scope of the variation power in the relevant trust deed, changes over time to the trust property and beneficiaries should not trigger a resettlement, provided that they can be identified at all times and there has not been a severance which would lead to the termination of the trust.

Following the withdrawal of its SOP, the ATO released TD 2012/21. This determination states the ATO's position formerly set out in its SOP was unsustainable following the court's decision in *Clark* and that:

> *"Neither CGT event E1 nor CGT event E2 ... happens unless:*
>
> - *the change causes the existing trust to terminate and a new trust to arise for trust law purposes, or*

- *the effect of the change ... is such as to lead to a particular asset being subject to a separate charter of rights and obligations such as to give rise to the conclusion that that asset has been settled on terms of a different trust.*"

Following the court's decision in *Clark* and the subsequent removal of the *ATO's SOP*, the risk of a resettlement on a trust split has clearly reduced. When structuring splitting transaction, however, it is arguably still the case that:

a the trustee indemnity provisions should be retained;

b no steps should be taken towards limiting the range of beneficiaries entitled to the assets of the trust, and in particular:

  (i) no steps be taken by particular beneficiaries to renounce their entitlements in respect of the assets held in the split trust or the original trust; and

  (i) no agreements should be made in respect of future distributions from the split trust or the original trust, ie the trustee of each trust should retain full discretion as to distributions in each year; and

c the trust deed should contain an express power permitting a separate trustee to be appointed to particular trust assets. As set out above, for testamentary trusts, this aspect may be particularly difficult to address, unless the relevant powers are in the will before the will maker dies.

Bespoke trustee company constitutions

As mentioned earlier in this article, one of the critical aspects of any estate planning exercise is determining what assets will in fact form part of the personal wealth to be distributed under a will. Set out below are specific comments in relation to the way in which personally owned assets can be controlled via tailored trustee company constitutions, where those companies are appointed as trustees for a testamentary trust. Virtually all of the comments are equally applicable to similar style control mechanisms for preexisting discretionary trusts. Therefore, although the article will focus on testamentary trusts, many of the principles are likely to be relevant for similar trust structures established during a will maker's lifetime.

Control of testamentary trusts

Control of a testamentary trust will usually rest with two key roles, namely:

a the trustee; and

b the appointor (sometimes referred to as the principal, guardian, nominator or protector), if such a position exists.

The transfer of control of a testamentary trust can generally be dealt with through:

a providing for the succession of the role of appointor or individual trustee (if applicable), and in this regard, reviewing the terms of the will is imperative to ensure that control of the trust passes to the intended and appropriate successor or successors;

b transferring the shares in a corporate trustee (including the possibility of a share split in the corporate trustee); and
c careful drafting of the constitution or shareholders' agreement (if one exists) of the corporate trustee (where applicable).

"Corporatising" a discretionary trust

It is possible to provide for quasi corporatisation of a testamentary trust by appointing a corporate trustee and implementing a number of control mechanisms in the governing documentation of the company, for example a shareholders' agreement or bespoke company constitution.

It is generally accepted that it is not possible for a beneficiary of a testamentary trust to prescribe how the trustee can exercise its discretion, as this will contravene the fundamental principle of trust law that the discretion of a trustee of a discretionary trust cannot be fettered.

However, it is possible to utilise the rules in the *Corporations Act 2001* (Cth) (Corporations Act) as they apply to the corporate trustee to implement a specific framework in which the trustee can operate. This framework is often outlined in the constitution for the corporate trustee, or in a shareholders' agreement, which will often operate in conjunction with an interfamily agreement or a family constitution.

By inserting control mechanisms in the governing documents for a corporate trustee, it is possible to create specific levels of control over the trust and to ensure that the controllers of the trust exercise their discretion in a manner which is consistent with the family succession strategy.

Corporations Act

The Corporations Act provides that a company's constitution is a contract between the directors and the company (ie the members). Section 136(2) of the Corporations Act permits a constitution to impose additional obligations on directors and members, in addition to the requirements set out in the Corporations Act, provided that the constitution only varies the replaceable rules.

Generally, the director and decision-making control mechanisms hardwired into a bespoke constitution will only alter the replaceable rules, and as such, should be valid under the Corporations Act.

Further, the sections in the Corporations Act governing the transfer of shares are also replaceable rules, and therefore any requirements in a constitution confirming, for example, that a member may only transfer their shares to their lineal descendants will be valid under the Corporations Act.

Examples of control mechanisms which may be appropriate to include in a bespoke trustee company constitution:

a specifying how shareholder and director decisions should be made, including for example, that particular decisions may only be made by unanimous or special majority decision;
b a requirement that each shareholder should be entitled to appoint and remove a representative director;
c restrictions on the transfer of shares;
d restrictions on the class of people entitled to be a shareholder or director, for example limiting shareholders to lineal descendants of nominated family members;
e naming of specific successor directors upon the occurrence of specified events;
f the involvement of any independent (ie non-family) advisers in the management of the company and the extent of their involvement; and
g any triggers for the transition of control to particular people, for example, on family members reaching a specified age.

Achieving certainty in relation to distributions of wealth (ie trust distributions) is often an important part of the family succession strategy and this can be addressed in a number of ways, for example:

a inserting a distribution policy into an interfamily agreement or a family constitution, shareholders' agreement or constitution — for example, formulas or specific guidelines; or
b leaving discretion to the controllers of the wealth, but requiring that decisions in this regard be made unanimously, with reference to the guidance that is provided by, for example, a family council or professional advisers.

It is also necessary to ensure that the appointor roles align with the control mechanisms implemented for the corporate trustee. In some circumstances, it may be appropriate for the appointor provisions to be removed completely to centralise control with the corporate trustee, determined by its shareholding. In other circumstances, it may be appropriate to retain the appointor role and ensure that the succession of this role is "hardwired" into the terms of the will.

Where there are joint appointors, it is important to review the decision-making mechanisms and ensure that these align with the approach implemented at the trustee level. Where the appointor is a natural person, it is critical to understand how the will provides for the succession of this role on death or incapacity.

Domicile

As mentioned earlier in this article, stamp duty exemption from a true "cloning" perspective is only available in Queensland. Similarly, South Australia is unique currently as it is the only Australian jurisdiction that has effectively abolished the rule against perpetuities.

The question as to whether the controllers of a testamentary trust can "forum shop" the jurisdiction that they wish to be subject to is an area of some uncertainty. The main issues that would need to be considered are as follows:

a it is generally accepted that in order for a trustee to change the relevant jurisdiction, it must have the power to do so under the trust instrument;

b as mentioned above, given many testamentary trusts do not have any power to vary, this may in a practical sense, prevent a change of relevant law;

c in relation to the changing of jurisdiction to South Australia for perpetuity periods, in addition to the variation to change the relevant law, it would also be necessary in most testamentary trust instruments to formally amend the vesting date definition — again this may be prohibited for the reasons outlined above;

d even if a testamentary trust has a power to vary, it may be that a purported attempt to change the relevant law is held to be invalid on public policy grounds or, alternatively, due to the various rules prohibiting the delegation of testamentary powers;

e there remains some residual risk, despite Clark, that any change of relevant law may of itself (or when combined with other changes) constitute a resettlement for CGT purposes of the trust;

f depending on the underlying assets of the relevant trust, any purported change to the relevant law may not provide the intended benefits. For example, if there is a desire to transfer real property under a trust clone and that real property is located outside Queensland, even if the testamentary trust is regulated by Queensland laws there will still be an obligation to arrange for stamping in the jurisdiction the property is physically located; and

g this said, the practical restrictions on changing jurisdiction may not be as problematic in relation to trusts seeking to be subject to South Australian law for perpetuity purposes, although the issue in this regard remains largely untested.

Conclusion

In many respects, the ability to use creative planning for testamentary trusts is analogous to similar strategies for any other form of trust. There are, however, some fundamental differences in the way testamentary trusts can be adjusted. It is therefore critical to adopt a methodical approach that addresses all potential issues.

Given the increasing prevalence of testamentary trusts in the estate planning process and the massive amount of wealth that is likely to be subject to intergenerational transfer over the next 20 years, the planning opportunities in relation to testamentary trusts will in all likelihood only continue to become increasingly important.

Matthew Burgess, CTA

Acknowledgment

Thank you for the contribution of the co-authors of the original articles.

Disclaimer

This article covers legal and technical issues in a general way. It is not designed to express opinions on specific cases. This article is intended for information purposes only and should not be regarded as legal advice. Further advice should be obtained before taking action on any issue dealt with in this document.

References

[1] 91 ATC 4007.

[2] *Bamford v FCT* [2010] HCA 10.

[3] S 118-195 ITAA 1997.

[4] S 118-125 ITAA97.

[5] S 104-55 ITAA97.

[6] S 128-15(3) ITAA97.

[7] S 128-15(5) ITAA97.

[8] S 128-15(3) ITAA97.

[9] M Blissenden, "Legislating ATO practice – the good and the bad for practitioners", (2013/2014) 48 *Taxation in Australia* 6.

[10] *FCT v Clark* [2011] FCAFC 5.

THE CLARK DECISION: POSSIBLE CONSEQUENCES FOR CGT EVENT E4?

Abstract

THE ARTICLE 'FIXED Trusts and Unit Trusts: One and the Same' in Volume 48(6), December 2013/January 2014 of the Journal considered a number of aspects in relation to fixed trusts and unit trusts. A number of members contacted the authors in relation to the comments that capital gains tax (**CGT**) event E4 should only apply to fixed trusts, and by implication, not unit trusts. This article explores the various issues in this regard.

CGT event E4

While a landmark decision in relation to CGT event E1 and the concept of trust resettlements, the decision of *Commissioner of Taxation v Clark*[1] (**Clark**) also has potential consequences for CGT event E4.

CGT event E4 happens if:

a the trustee of a trust makes a payment to a taxpayer in respect of a unit or interest in the trust (except for CGT event A1, C2, E1, E2, E6 or E7 happening in relation to it); and

b some or all of the payment (the non-assessable part) is not included in the taxpayer's assessable income.[2]

It is clear that CGT event E4 applies to unit trusts and fixed trusts, due to the express words in section 104-70(1) '*in respect of your unit or interest in the trust*'.

However, the ATO has provided clarification in Tax Determination (**TD**) 2003/28 about the meaning of the words '*interest in the trust*' in section 104-70(1), stating:

> *'The meaning to be given to the words 'interest in the trust' depends on the context in which they are used, see for example Leedale v. Lewis [1982] 3 All ER 808 and Gartside v. IRC [1968] AC 553. In its context in section 104-70, the interest in the trust is one that is coloured by the nature of a unit in a unit trust, that is, the interest in the trust is one that is akin to the interest that a unit holder has in a unit trust. The interest that is contemplated is one in which a taxpayer invests.*[3]'

TD 2003/28 confirms that CGT event E4 does not apply where a beneficiary's interest is that of a mere object in a discretionary trust, even if the beneficiary has an interest in default of appointment.[4]

In light of the comments in TD 2003/28, there has been some uncertainty as to the application of CGT event E4 to an interest in a 'hybrid' trust (for example, a unit trust where beneficiaries have both fixed and discretionary entitlements).[5]

The National Tax Liaison Group subcommittee minutes from the meeting on 11 June 2003 (**NTLG minutes**) indicate that CGT event E4 will not apply in the case of a unit trust, even where there are discretionary units (for example, a hybrid trust). This conclusion is based on the Australian Taxation Office's (**ATO**) reasoning in TD 97/15W (the predecessor to TD 2003/28) that CGT event E4 does not apply to a non-assessable payment made by a trustee to a beneficiary of a discretionary trust.

In particular, the NTLG minutes state:

'a non-assessable amount paid to the owners of discretionary 'special units' is not a payment of the type contemplated by section 104-70 of the ITAA 1997. Therefore CGT event E4 will not happen when such payment is made to the owners of special units that only have a discretionary entitlement to capital contributions. A beneficiary with only a discretionary interest in a trust does not own an interest in the trust that is of the nature or character contemplated by section 104-70 of the ITAA 1997.'

The NTLG minutes refer to TD 97/15 which was withdrawn after the NTLG minutes were released, and effectively replaced with TD 2003/28. The notice of withdrawal for TD 97/15 confirms that the views of the ATO expressed in TD 2003/28 are the same as those in TD 97/15 in respect of the mere objects of a trust. Therefore, the withdrawal of TD 97/15 should not alter the effect of the comments in the NTLG minutes.

Notwithstanding the phrase 'unit or interest in the trust' in section 104-70, the NTLG minutes and various private rulings issued by the ATO (for example, private ruling 26597) confirm that the mere label in a trust instrument of an interest as a 'unit' is not sufficient for CGT event E4 to apply. Instead, the relevant consideration is whether the units or interest create particular entitlements that sufficiently satisfy the provisions in section 104-70.

While the NTLG minutes are obviously not binding on the question of whether CGT event E4 can apply to a unit trust where the unitholders have discretionary entitlements, the comments do assist with the ATO's likely interpretation of section 104-70 particularly when read in conjunction with the guidance in TD 2003/28.

The recent article 'Payment of non-assessable amount to an owner of discretionary units and CGT event E4' provides further examination of the ATO guidance in this regard.[6]

The Clark decision

There have been numerous articles published in the Taxation Institute of Australia Journal about the Clark decision, and this article therefore does not set out an in-depth analysis of the case.

However, briefly, in Clark the Full Court of the Federal Court effectively confirmed that there is a very wide ability to amend a trust deed without causing a resettlement, provided the amendment is within the scope of the variation power under the trust instrument.

The Clark case involved a unit trust which had been substantially varied over several years. Some of the variations included the changing of the trustee, the beneficiaries and the trust property. The Court rejected the ATO's argument that these amendments had amounted to a resettlement of the trust, stating that a resettlement will not occur where there has been continuity of:

a the terms of the trust deed;
b the trust property; and
c the membership of the trust.

The Court also confirmed that where variations are within the scope of a variation power in the relevant trust deed, changes over time to the trust property and beneficiaries should not trigger a resettlement, provided that they can be identified at all times and there has not been a severance which would lead to the termination of the trust.

The ATO has accepted in TD 2012/21 that a valid amendment to a trust not resulting in a termination of the trust will not of itself result in the happening of CGT event E1.

Possible consequences for CGT event E4 following Clark

Following the Clark decision, it is arguably possible to vary a trust deed to limit the impact of CGT event E4 in circumstances where the trust in question is not a fixed trust.

In particular, where a unit trust deed contains an adequate variation power, the rights of the unitholders could be varied to create a discretionary entitlement, such that the trust will effectively become a hybrid trust, with both fixed and discretionary entitlements. Applying the principles from the Clark decision, this style of variation should not trigger a resettlement of the trust.

In turn, applying the guidance provided in the NTLG Minutes and TD 2003/28, CGT event E4 should then not apply in relation to payments made via the discretionary entitlements. That is, where a unitholder's entitlement to a payment is at the discretion of the trustee, CGT event E4 will not be relevant.

As set out in the recent article 'Fixed Trusts and Unit Trusts: One and the Same'[7], following the Colonial decision[8], a trust will be a fixed trust for taxation purposes where beneficiaries (or unitholders) have a vested and indefeasible interest in the trust. It is generally accepted that a fixed trust will exist if a trust deed has the following provisions:

a the trustee cannot create different rights or different classes of units;
b all units on issue must have the same rights to receive income and capital of the trust;
c all units must be allotted for market value;

d all income and capital of the trust must be distributed in proportion to the unit holdings, i.e. there is no discretion held by the trustee and in particular there must be no discretionary elements that may mean the trust is a 'hybrid' trust;
e partly paid units cannot be issued;

f the trust deed must require all unitholders to agree on the redemption of units and any redemption must be at market value;
g all valuations of the trust fund, and in turn the determination of unit values, must be conducted by a valuer in accordance with 'applicable Australian accounting principles';
h the trustee cannot make gifts; and
i the unanimous consent of all unitholders must be required to vary the trust deed, however there must be a complete prohibition in the variation power ensuring that no amendments can be made in relation to any of the above provisions.

Conclusion

Where a trust satisfies the definition of a fixed trust, or has a prohibition on variation similar to that outlined above, there will be no ability to leverage off the Clark decision to minimise the potential application of CGT event E4.

Given the observation in Colonial that very few trusts are likely to satisfy the definition of a fixed trust, prudence would dictate considering the impact of the Clark decision in the context of any trust to which CGT event E4 may otherwise apply to.

That said, it is also important to consider all consequences of varying a non-fixed trust deed in a manner that may limit the operation of CGT event E4, for example:

a this type of approach is unlikely to be commercially appropriate where the units are held by arm's length parties;

b the impact of any interest deductions where unitholders have borrowed funds to acquire the units would need to be considered; and
c the application of Part IVA *Income Tax Assessment Act 1936* (Cth) must always be analysed.

References

[1] [2011] FCAFC 5.

[2] *Section 104-70(1) Income Tax Assessment Act 1997 (Cth).*

[3] Paragraph 4 TD 2003/28.

[4] Paragraph 3 TD 2003/28

[5] "Payment of a non-assessable amount to an owner of discretionary units and CGT event E4" Volume 48(3), September 2013, Taxation in Australia;
"Does CGT event C2 apply when a beneficiary's interest in a trust ends?" Volume 48(6), December 2013/January 2014 Taxation in Australia.

[6] Payment of a non-assessable amount to an owner of discretionary units and CGT event E4" Volume 48(3), September 2013, Taxation in Australia.

[7] Volume 48(6), December 2013/January 2014 Taxation in Australia.

[8] [2011] FCA 16.

BUST PROOFING TRUSTS

As PREVIOUS ARTICLES have highlighted, the need for effective structuring of business and personal assets has been brought into sharp focus for high net wealth individuals and business owners in recent years.

In particular, the potential ineffectiveness of trust structures has been highlighted by a myriad of court decisions and legislative changes since 2010.

This article explores the key issues to consider when seeking to 'bust-proof' a trust in broadly the following order:

(1) The consequences of recent family court decisions involving trusts;
(2) Some practical recommendations when dealing with trusts in the context of structuring a client's affairs;
(3) The impact of the decision in Australian Securities and Investments Commission in the Matter of Richstar Enterprises Pty Ltd (ACN 099 071 968) v Carey (No 6)[1] (Richstar);
(4) The Bankruptcy Act 1966 (Cth) (Bankruptcy Act); and
(5) Some critical issues to consider whenever establishing or amending a trust deed.

While the impact of the family court decisions on trusts is obviously significant, this article only focuses on decisions since the publication in this journal of our detailed article "Trust assets and estate planning: how has the dust settled after Kennon v Spry[2]" (**Spry**).

Overview

The asset protection typically understood to be afforded by trusts is derived from the longstanding view that a mere discretionary beneficiary of a trust does not have a proprietary interest in a trust's assets, and the main right of a discretionary beneficiary is limited to enforcing due administration by the trustee. Consequently it is difficult to value this right when the beneficiary has no present entitlement to the trust's assets and may never have any entitlement to any part of the income or capital of the discretionary trust.

While this has been the accepted view for hundreds of years, recent decisions in Australia potentially undermine the level of asset protection afforded by trusts.

The high profile decision of Richstar considered whether a beneficiary can have a proprietary interest in the assets of a trust where that beneficiary has 'effective control' over the trust.

In Richstar, the Court held that some of the defendants had 'at least a contingent interest' in the trust property, which was sufficient for the property to be potentially available to the receivers. A contingent interest was found to arise where 'the trustee is effectively the alter ego of the relevant beneficiary or otherwise subject to his or its effective control'.

Although the Court did not allow the full order sought by the ASIC, the decision challenged the traditional view that for a beneficiary of a discretionary trust mere 'expectancy' is not sufficient to constitute 'property' which is available to creditors.

For completeness, it should be noted that Richstar was a decision about proprietary interests in a bankruptcy context.

Family law considerations

Overview

As explained in detail in the author's earlier article[3], initially the Spry[4] decision raised concerns that it effectively created a significant widening of the Courts' power to effectively disregard the existence of a trust when considering the division of assets on a property settlement.

Over time, the practical impact of the decision has arguably softened, not least of which due to the fact that the outcome of the decision appears to be strongly linked to the somewhat unique circumstances of the case.

In particular, the arguably questionable conduct by the husband (such as mismanagement of trust assets, threatened destruction of trust assets, misleading representations to the Courts and attempted direct communication with the judges) may have contributed significantly to the outcome.

A number of cases since 2008 reinforce the conclusion that the impact of Spry has not been as severe as initially feared. Aside from the numerous cases analysed in the author's earlier article, there have also been a number of recent family court cases that are directly relevant to the ability to structure trusts robustly.

A number of the key cases in this regard are summarised below.

Family courts' power to adjust inheritance rights

Arguably the most widely published case since Spry was the High Court judgment of Stanford v Stanford[5] (**Stanford**) where the Family Courts' powers to potentially displace the distribution of assets under an estate plan that involved a form of trust (namely a life estate) were analysed.

The brief facts were that Mr and Mrs Stanford had no children together, although both had children from previous relationships. The Stanford's had both crafted their estate plans to provide for their respective children, without making provision for each other, other than a life tenancy in the family home. The house was owned solely in the name of Mr Stanford (he had bought it before the marriage), although it had been lived in by the couple for over 40 years.

Critically, Mrs Stanford appointed her children, not Mr Stanford, under her guardian and attorney documents.

Due to ill health and mental incapacity, Mrs Stanford was moved into residential care. Despite no suggestion that the couple were anything other than happily married, on her mother's incapacity Mrs Stanford's daughter initiated proceedings in the Family Court (as Mrs Stanford's legal guardian) seeking orders for equal division of the marital property (the main asset was the family home) between Mr and Mrs Stanford.

The initial Judge ordered that Mr Stanford pay a fixed sum of approximately half the value of the marital property to Mrs Stanford, which payment would have effectively passed directly to her guardians. To fund the payment the family home would have needed to be sold, forcing Mr Stanford to leave the house.

Mr Stanford appealed the decision, however Mrs Stanford passed away before judgment was delivered by the Court of Appeal. The Court of Appeal ultimately decided that Mrs Stanford's legal personal representatives should receive the fixed sum upon the death of Mr Stanford. This decision effectively altered the distribution of Mr Stanford's estate (which Mrs Stanford had agreed with while she had capacity) under his will as the house (following his wife's death) would have otherwise passed to his children.

The decision of the Court of Appeal was ultimately set aside on appeal to the High Court, on the basis that the order was not just and equitable. However, importantly, the High Court confirmed that the death of a party to a marriage 'does not transform the nature of the claim (for example, into a claim by the beneficiaries of the wife's estate)'.

In other words, the right of a guardian or attorney to commence property settlement proceedings was effectively confirmed, even where (as here) they would have no entitlement to challenge the estate of their stepfather.

Asking the right questions

Beeson v Spence[6] (**Beeson**) highlights the importance of the factual matrix on how exposed the assets of a trust are in a family law context.

The wife and the husband met in 1996 in this case and married in 1997. They had two children and subsequently divorced in 2004. In 2001 the wife had established a trust known as the S Trust.

On establishment of the trust, the wife's father and her solicitor were appointed as trustees and the wife was the appointor. The specified beneficiaries were the two children of the marriage and the wife and husband were within the class of potential beneficiaries.

In 2003, at a time when the husband was going through financial difficulties, and when the wife and husband had separated, the deed was varied to exclude the wife and the husband as potential beneficiaries of the trust, as well as to resign the wife as appointor. A new appointor, being the wife's sister, was nominated in her place.

After the variation the deed practically still entitled the wife and husband to receive distributions, not as potential beneficiaries, but as 'parents' of the children who remained specified beneficiaries.

In the property settlement proceedings, the husband argued that the trust was established for the benefit of the family as a whole and not just the children. In contrast, the wife suggested that the trust was ultimately established for the purpose of benefitting the children of the relationship and therefore the assets should not be treated as property of the marriage.

Having reviewed all of the available facts, the Court ignored the release of direct control by the wife (through her resignation as the appointor and the removal of beneficiaries) and held that the wife still retained sufficient control of the trust to support a conclusion that the assets should be treated as property of the marriage.

Some of the key questions the court in Beeson took into account when deciding the assets of the trust were property of the marriage are set out below.

Who is the trustee of the trust?

The trustees of the trust were the wife's father and her solicitor. They had the discretion to administer the trust.

Does the trust deed restrict the range of beneficiaries who can receive income or capital distributions?

The specified beneficiaries were the children of the husband and wife, and the husband and wife were initially potential beneficiaries as parents of the specified beneficiaries. By the deed of variation (instigated by the wife) in 2003 the husband and wife were removed as potential beneficiaries. After the deed of variation the wife and husband were entitled to receive distributions, not as potential beneficiaries, but as 'parents' of the specified beneficiaries.

Does the trustee need consent/approval of any other person for distribution?

No. However, the trust deed gave the wife ultimate control of the distribution of income and capital by giving her power of appointment and removal of trustee, who in turn had the discretion to distribute to the wife and the husband to the exclusion of the children. This level of control pointed towards the trust being an alter ego of the wife, and the conclusion that the assets were property of the marriage, not the children.

Does the trustee effectively/practically control the trust in an unfettered way?

No. Up until her resignation under the deed of variation in 2003, the wife as appointor had complete control over the appointment and removal of the trustee. The consent of the appointor was required for the trustee to vary the terms of the trust deed. Nothing, including a request by the trustee, obliged the wife as appointor to relinquish control of the Trust.

Does the trustee exercise its powers independently or are they controlled or subject to approval by any other person or entity?

While the trustee had the discretion to make distributions, the power to vary the deed was subject to approval by the appointor and the appointor could remove the trustee at any time.

Can beneficiaries be removed or added, and if so by whom?

The beneficiaries could be removed or added by the trustees, only with the consent of the appointor.

Is there any risk that the trustee may be seen as simply the 'alter ego' of some other person?

The Court found that the trust was created with the wife in control of the appointment of those with the duty of administering it and it was never created to benefit the children alone. The assets of what was essentially a 'standard' discretionary trust were controlled by a party to property proceedings who ultimately had the power to legitimately determine at any point to whom income and/or capital was to be distributed, including herself.

Does someone (e.g. an appointor, guardian, principal) have the power to unilaterally change the trustee?

Yes. The appointor was the wife initially. Whilst she subsequently relinquished control and appointed her sister as replacement appointor in 2003, the steps taken via the deed of variation were seen as having been taken at the wife's direction. This conclusion pointed towards the trust being the alter ego of the wife, and thus the property of the marriage and not the property of the children.

If the appointor ceases to act, do their powers pass to anyone else, and if so, who?

The deed provided for the appointor powers to pass to Mr Beeson, the wife's father and trustee of the trust, upon her death. The deed also allowed for the wife as the original appointor to name a successor appointor (which she did, namely her sister).

For an existing trust, has there been a pattern of income or capital distributions?

Distributions were made from income in both 2002 and 2003 to the specified beneficiaries being the children. Distributions were also made to the wife in this period, which she applied, among other things, to payment of her legal costs. While the wife argued the legal costs incurred showed the fund was used for the children's benefit, it was held that the legal costs should be seen as being incurred on her own account. This supported the conclusion that the trust was not the sole benefit of the children.

Further, there was nothing improper about the trustees distributing funds in the wife's favour, as she was a potential beneficiary up until the variation in 2003, and continued to be entitled to receive distributions as a 'parent' of the specified beneficiaries after the variation.

Access to trust documents in Family Court cases

The case of Schweitzer & Schweitzer[7] considered the disclosure of documents claimed by one spouse to be in the possession, or under control, of the other.

The specific facts of this case were that the husband was a director of two corporate trustees, but not the sole director. In one corporate trustee, the husband's father was the other director. In the other corporate trustee, the husband's father and mother were the other directors.

While the husband was not a shareholder of either of the trustee companies, however he was a discretionary beneficiary of both trusts.

The appointor of both trusts was the husband's father.

The wife applied to the court asking that the husband disclose the financial statements, tax returns, bank statements and the minutes of meeting relating to trust distributions by the corporate trustees.

The wife's request was rejected on the grounds that the husband had a fiduciary obligation in relation to the holding and use of trust and corporate trustee documents.

The court also held that the documents were not under the husband's 'control' for the purpose of the Family Court rules. The decision confirms that directors of corporate trustees have no right to 'possession' or 'control', but only to 'access' trust documents and that such access must be used strictly for the trust or company purposes.

The documents might have been accessible if the wife was able to join the corporate trustees as parties to the proceedings, although this was not necessarily something the court would approve; and even if they were joined, disclosure of the documents would still be subject to the court's discretion.

In the case of MacDowell & Williams and Ors[8], the court denied the request for disclosure of the wills and documents relating to the corporate and trust structures of wife's parents.

The wife and the husband married in April 2004 and separated on a final basis on 12 July 2010. The husband had submitted that the documents requested were relevant to the marital property pool and in determining the financial resources available to the wife.

The wife's parents filed an objection to the husband's request on the basis that:

a the documents sought from them in their personal capacity were not relevant as they maintained testamentary capacity; and
b the documents sought from them in their capacity as directors were not relevant as neither the wife nor the husband had any proprietary interest.

In relation to the parents' wills, the court said the request was a 'fishing expedition' by the husband. Although there may be compelling circumstances which warrant the disclosure of will documents (for example, when a parent has lost capacity), here, both parents were alive, in good health and possessed full testamentary capacity.

In relation to the financial and corporate documents, it was held that there was no evidence to suggest that the wife had control over any of the entities, or that control was likely to arise in the future.

The court then considered the previous distributions of one trust where the wife was both the primary and default beneficiary. Given, however, that the wife had only received $28,000 over the ten years of the existence of the trust, and during that time, distributions had also been made to other beneficiaries of the trust, the court held that it was clearly 'discretionary' in nature.

The husband also sought to rely on purported interpretation of Spry and argue that the wife's interest in the trust were property, that being her 'right to consideration' and 'due administration'. The court held in favour of the wife's parents that this was a misstatement of the law on this point and that while such rights could be taken into account, they would generally be very difficult to value.

The court also bluntly distinguished Spry by noting that Dr Spry had total ultimate control of the trust in question, which was not the case here.

Similarly, the case of FCT & Darling and Anor[9] confirms that generally the Tax Office can only obtain information via Family Court proceedings if it demonstrates, on a case by case basis, that it is a person with "a proper interest" along with all of the reasons that support allowing such access.

In this case it was acknowledged that while the Tax Office does have special powers to obtain information to carry out its duties, this did not mean those powers could be used to undermine the preference of the Family Court to create an environment that encourages full and frank disclosure between former spouses.

Trusts and asset protection–protection from bankruptcy

Risk of claims by a trustee in bankruptcy

Where an individual or entity is involved in a profession or conducting a business, claims against them by creditors or potential litigants can expose all of the assets held.

The possibilities for litigation and claims by creditors against individuals to arise (and, therefore, also the potential for bankruptcy to occur) are numerous and include:

- claims against a business by their suppliers;
- product liability of manufacturing businesses;

- professional negligence claims against professionals (e.g. accountants, doctors, lawyers and financial advisers); and
- general negligence claims (e.g. operation of a motor vehicle causing personal or property damage).

There are also a number of potential risks of claims being made against directors of companies including personal liability for:

- the company's debts incurred in insolvent trading;
- some tax obligations of the company;
- unpaid employee's superannuation deductions;
- an ever widening statutory liability where directors are personally liable for the company's actions. Many State and Federal Acts impose this personal liability–one example is Workplace Health and Safety legislation;
- negligence; and
- guarantees.

Even relatively passive assets can result in litigation against the owner which brings with it the potential for bankruptcy. For example, a person who owns an investment property in their own name can be personally sued if a tenant trips and injures themselves on the property, subject to any insurance cover.

It is, therefore, vital to ensure that as many assets as possible are quarantined from an 'at risk' individual or entity to avoid them from being exposed to potential claims. It is also vital to ensure that assets with high risk exposure are quarantined from all other assets to limit the potential exposure to the value of those assets.

Movement into bankruptcy

Even if an individual or entity has caused litigation to arise, a lot must happen before a trustee in bankruptcy becomes involved. In summary, the steps are as follows:

- there must be a debt;
- if that debt is a judgment debt, there will have been a claim that has been successfully prosecuted in the courts;

- there must have been a failure to meet that debt; and
- the creditor must then have sought to appoint a trustee in bankruptcy to the debtor's estate. Depending on the circumstances, other arrangements might be considered to avoid the appointment of a trustee in bankruptcy. For example, the debtor might enter into an informal agreement with creditors, or enter into arrangements under Parts IX or X Bankruptcy Act.

A discussion of these various arrangements and options is outside the scope of this article, rather the focus here is the worst-case scenario, where a trustee in bankruptcy is appointed. However, the principles of protecting assets from exposure to claims against individuals are also relevant in the case of a scheme of arrangement.

Section 120, 121 and 122 'claw back' rules

In considering claims that might be brought by a trustee in bankruptcy, it is relevant to bear in mind the voidable transaction provisions in the Bankruptcy Act. These provisions, often referred to as 'claw back' provisions, enable the trustee in bankruptcy to trace and reclaim assets that were transferred prior to a person becoming bankrupt.

In particular, a transfer can be overturned, subject to certain exclusions:

- if the transfer took place within two years before the commencement of the bankruptcy where no consideration was paid or where consideration was less than market value (section 120(3) Bankruptcy Act)–or four years for related entities;
- if the transfer took place within five years before the commencement of the bankruptcy and at the time of the transfer the person was insolvent, where no consideration was paid or where consideration was less than market value (section 120(1) Bankruptcy Act);
- if the transfer took place within six months before the commencement of the bankruptcy, the transfer is to a creditor, the creditor obtains a preference, priority or advantage over other creditors and

at the time of the transfer the transferor was insolvent (section 122 Bankruptcy Act); or

- at any time where the main purpose in making the transfer is to prevent the transferred property from becoming divisible, or to hinder or to delay the process of making property available for division, among creditors (section 121(1) Bankruptcy Act).

As the commencement of the bankruptcy may be dated from the first act of bankruptcy within the six months before a relevant petition was presented, up to a further six months could be added to these periods of 'claw back'.

It is significant to note that, if sections 120 and 121 void (claw back) the transfer of property, there is a requirement to pay to the transferee the consideration (if any) that they had paid.

These provisions pose a potential threat to the whole strategy of accumulating assets in the hands of 'low risk' entities, where value must be 'moved' (a financial contribution) to that 'low risk' entity.

Ultimately, in any asset protection exercise, the impact of the 'claw-back' rules under the bankruptcy legislation needs to be carefully considered.

Probably the fundamental aspect in this regard is whether a decision by a person to divest themselves of assets was done for the main purpose of defeating creditors.

The leading case in this area arguably remains Williams v Lloyd[10].

In this case, a bankrupt transferred assets to family members while he was solvent, but knowing that he was likely to start engaging in a 'risky' business activity in the future.

The court held that the transfers could not be clawed back and the key aspect of the decision was as follows:

> 'Once it is acknowledged, as upon the evidence I think it must be, that in 1926 the bankrupt was in a perfectly sound financial position and had nothing to fear, subsequent conduct and events form an insufficient basis for a finding that the documents were shams, or that he had an intent to defraud his creditors, or that they were made

subject to a suspensory condition allowing them to take effect only in case of attack by creditors'.

Bankruptcy issues with trusts

Vesting of property upon bankruptcy

Generally, the property of the bankrupt vests in the trustee in bankruptcy as and from the commencement of the bankruptcy.

However, subject to the comments below, the property of the bankrupt does not include the assets of a trust of which they are a discretionary object. The primary reason for this is that no beneficiaries of a trust have any defined interest in the trust assets, but rather merely have a right to have the trust administered in accordance with the terms of the trust established under the deed (Gartside v Inland Revenue Commissioners[11]).

Therefore, if a beneficiary becomes bankrupt, the assets of the trust will not be available to their creditors unless the trustee makes a distribution to that beneficiary.

This general position is subject to a number of possible exceptions, including:

- flow through of income;
- exposing the assets of the trust;
- 'beneficiary loan accounts' or other debts owed by the trustee to a bankrupt beneficiary;
- where the bankrupt is a default beneficiary;
- where the 'at risk' beneficiary is the appointor/principal; and
- where the 'at risk' beneficiary is the trustee.

Each of these issues will be dealt with in turn below, before the implications of the Richstar decision are considered in detail.

Flow through of income

Income derived by a trust will usually flow through to the beneficiaries by force of tax pressure. This is to ensure that the trustee is not assessed at the top marginal tax rate under section 99A Income Tax Assessment Act 1936 on any undistributed income.

Beneficiaries will be presently entitled to income, which is appointed or applied to them by the trustee. Clearly, where a beneficiary who has a vested interest because the trustee exercises its discretion to vest income (or indeed capital) in the beneficiary, that interest will be exposed to a claim against the beneficiary.

A simple solution would be for the trustee to exercise its discretionary power to distribute the share of the income for any year where a beneficiary is bankrupt to beneficiaries who are themselves not at risk.

Other solutions may include:

- establishing separate or sub trusts in relation to income to which beneficiaries other than the bankrupt are presently entitled. In either case, the amounts distributed to those trusts will be liabilities in which the trustee in bankruptcy will have no priority; or
- ensuring that the terms of the trust prohibit the trustees from distributing income and capital to the 'at risk' beneficiary.

Invalid distributions

In the context of trust distributions, the "read the deed" mantra is well known.

The family law case of Harris v Harris[12] is one example of a situation that turned in part on the range of potential beneficiaries.

In that case, the trial judge in a family court matter noted that the recipient of trust distributions (being a company), who was being challenged, was not in fact an eligible beneficiary of the relevant trust. If the company had been simply nominated as a potential beneficiary, then the distributions would have most likely been valid.

A more common example of where difficulties with invalid distributions arise, however, relates to where particular potential beneficiaries are in fact expressly excluded by the trust deed. The most common example in this regard is the exclusion of the trustee, be that the current, former or even a future trustee, from being a beneficiary of a trust.

These types of clauses are often found in deeds prepared by New South Wales advisers. This is primarily because s 54(3) of the Duties Act 1997 (NSW) limits the nominal duty exemption for a change of trustee to trust deeds that contain provisions ensuring that:

(1) none of the continuing trustees remaining after the appointment of a new trustee are or can become a beneficiary under the trust;
(2) none of the trustees of the trust after the appointment of a new trustee are or can become a beneficiary under the trust; and
(3) the transfer is not part of a scheme for conferring an interest, in relation to the trust property, on a new trustee or any other person, whether as a beneficiary or otherwise, to the detriment of the beneficial interest or potential beneficial interest of any person.

An example of a clause adopting an approach that ensures access to the stamp duty relief is as follows:

> 'The Trustee for the time being of the Trust cannot be a beneficiary of the Trust. None of the continuing Trustees remaining after the retirement of a Trustee is or can become a beneficiary under the Trust, and none of the Trustees of the Trust after the appointment of a new Trustee is or can become a beneficiary under the Trust.'

New South Wales is the only Australian jurisdiction that has this type of restriction on accessing the duty concessions for a change of trustee and, understandably, clauses drafted in this manner are extremely prevalent with deed providers or lawyers based in New South Wales.

In many instances, however, there may in fact be no other connection with New South Wales for anyone associated with the trust.

The risks created by this drafting approach will, therefore, often be less than obvious. Anecdotally, there would seem to be an increasing number of situations where invalid distributions are being discovered that stretch back over many years and involve significant levels of invalid distributions. The exact ramifications of this type of situation will depend on a range of issues, including how any default provision under the relevant trust deed is crafted.

Tax Office tracing of trust distributions

On stark example of the Tax Office's attitude towards trust distributions is its review around identification of beneficiaries of certain distributions, particularly where trust to trust distributions are involved.

In particular, trustees are required to complete an Ultimate Beneficiary Statement where a distribution is made to another trust, failing which ultimate beneficiary non-disclosure tax is imposed on the trustee of the original trust equal to the highest marginal tax rate plus the Medicare levy.

Following the 2013 Federal Budget, the Tax Office also announced details of the 'Trusts Taskforce' which, in addition to the stated goal of identifying 'egregious tax avoidance and evasion using trust structures' is stated to be focused on:

a unregistered trusts and their beneficiaries;
b trusts that are irregular in lodging tax returns;
c offshore trust dealings involving secrecy jurisdictions;
d sham transactions; and
e artificial re-characterisation of amounts.

The Tax Office has however stated that the intended targets of the Taskforce are high risk taxpayers and not ordinary arrangements and tax planning associated with genuine business or family dealings.

Exposing the assets of the trust

It is important to remember that using a trust does not magically confer protection to the assets of the trust. The assets of the trust can easily be exposed within the trust environment. In particular, where the trustees carry on a business or apply the assets to other high risk activities.

Ideally, therefore, trusts should be utilised solely for passive investments or alternatively sub trusts or separate structures should be used to quarantine more risky activities.

Beneficiary Loan Accounts

The balance of 'beneficiary loan accounts' should be reviewed regularly which have built up as a result of tax distributions not being matched by cash payments out of the trust.

Any credit beneficiary loan accounts are an asset of the beneficiary, and thus are exposed to any claim brought against the beneficiary. It is important to ensure that trustees do not create beneficiary loan accounts in beneficiaries with a high level of exposure.

It is also unwise to have 'at risk' beneficiaries lending back distributions received to the trust, which also leads to the creation (and accumulation) of a loan account in favour of the beneficiary with the trust.

It is important to ensure that beneficiaries with a level of exposure properly deal with loan accounts on an ongoing basis, particularly having regard to claw back provisions of the Bankruptcy Act set out above which could mean that the assets of the trust still remain exposed four years or more after a beneficiary gifts a previously created loan account back to the trust.

Default beneficiaries

Most trusts include default provisions in relation to both income and capital. That is, if the trustee fails to effectively exercise its discretion to distribute income in any year or capital on the trust vesting date, the trustee will be deemed to hold the undistributed income or capital for nominated default beneficiaries.

Some commentators have argued that the interest of these default beneficiaries constitutes property which may vest in the trustee in bankruptcy if a default beneficiary is declared bankrupt.

It has generally been argued that the interest of default beneficiaries is of a different character to that of a discretionary object and may well be property of a bankrupt (Dwyer v Ross[13]).

However, it has also been argued that the interests of takers in default do not have a vested interest in the assets of the trust until the trust vests and until that event occurs the assets of the trust have not been the subject of an effective appointment. That is, such interests can be deferred or taken away at any time prior to vesting or termination of the trust and accordingly such interests are 'mere expectancies' in respect of property which is not capable of vesting in a trustee in bankruptcy.

The preferred position adopted by the cases (despite the Richstar decision) remains that a default beneficiary does not have an interest in trust assets that amounts to property that is attackable by a trustee in bankruptcy.

This said, it is always appropriate when establishing a trust to consider carefully who should be nominated as the default beneficiaries to ensure that the assets of the trust do not become unnecessarily exposed to claims against those beneficiaries if the law in this area changes.

Powers of Appointor/Principal

Many trusts create a position for an appointor or principal who generally has the power of removal and appointment of the trustee.

A question that often arises is, whether, if a principal/appointor is subsequently declared bankrupt, is their power of appointment a 'property' which vests in and can be exercised by the trustee in bankruptcy?

The property of a bankrupt which is available for distribution to creditors includes 'the capacity to exercise, and to take proceedings for exercising, all such powers in, over or in respect of property as might have been exercised by the bankrupt for his own benefit ... ' (see section 116(1)(b) of the Bankruptcy Act).

However, it has been held that the right of a bankrupt to exercise a power of appointment under a discretionary trust is not property of the bankrupt (Re Burton; ex parte Wily v Burton[14])

Further, the decision in Dwyer v Ross suggests that a trustee in bankruptcy cannot compel the trustee of a trust to exercise the trustee's discretion in favour of a bankrupt beneficiary. To do so, could be construed as a breach of the trustee's duty to the solvent beneficiaries of the trust. It would be against the interests of the beneficiaries as a whole to exercise the power in that way. As a practical matter, however, if a trustee in bankruptcy purports to act in that way, the beneficiary and trustee is left to take action against the trustee which on a number of levels (not least of which being financial capacity) may not be possible.

Again, however, with reference to the principles following Richstar case outlined below it may still be prudent to ensure that:

- there are at least two persons filling the appointor/principal role, who must act jointly;
- any appointor/principal can resign; and
- any appointor/principal is automatically removed if declared bankrupt

Appointor succession

There does not necessarily need to be an appointor provision under a trust deed, however where there is, a trust deed will normally set out in some detail the way in which the role of appointor is dealt with on the death or incapacity of the person (or people) originally appointed.

Failing to understand succession arrangements of an appointor can create a range of difficulties as highlighted in the case of Montevento Holdings Pty Ltd v Scaffidi[15].

The case concerned a challenge by a beneficiary of a discretionary trust to a change of trustee by the appointor. The challenging beneficiary was Guiseppe Scaffidi who, along with Maria (his mother) and

Eugenio (his brother), was within the range of potential beneficiaries of the Scaffidi Family Trust.

The original appointor of the trust was Antonio Scaffidi (the father). On Antonio's death, Maria became the appointor and by deed Maria subsequently appointed Eugenio Scaffidi as the appointor.

After his appointment, Eugenio appointed Montevento Holdings Pty Ltd (a company of which he was the sole director and shareholder) as the sole trustee, effectively giving him complete control over the trust and its assets.

Guiseppe's challenge to the appointment of the trustee company ultimately failed before the High Court, essentially because the appointment complied with the provisions of the trust deed. The decision highlights that the role of appointor can often give ultimate control of a trust.

The relevant clause in this case precluded individual appointors from personally being appointed as trustee. However, the individual appointor appointed a company as trustee of which he was personally the sole director and shareholder.

The High Court held that the ordinary and natural meaning of the clause was that an individual person holding the office of appointor could not personally appoint themselves as trustee. As the trust deed consistently distinguished between individuals and companies, it did not prohibit the appointment of a corporate trustee, even if that trustee was controlled by the individual appointor.

Powers of Trustees

Similar to an appointor or principal, the trustee's powers may be available for distribution for creditors and therefore a similar approach to the appointor/principal should be adopted to minimise the risk for a trustee of the trust

Especially in circumstances where a beneficiary under a trust is also appointed as a trustee, it is generally sensible to appoint multiple trustees to act jointly with the beneficiary and may include a:

- family member,

- family friend,
- trustee company; or
- a combination of the above.

Alternatively, as mentioned above, (in relation to an appointor/principal) the trust may contain a clause that automatically removes the trustee if they are declared bankrupt.

Share self-ownership

Whenever reviewing existing structures or establishing new entities, reference to the Corporations Act 2001 is important. In particular, the Act expressly prohibits companies from owning shares in themselves.

This can arise in instances where a trustee company is incorrectly established with the trust (for which it is trustee) owning some or all of the shares. As the legal owner of those shares is the trustee, this results in the trustee owning shares in itself.

The relevant section is s 259A, which provides as follows:

'A company must not acquire shares (or units of shares) in itself except:

a in buying back shares under section 257A; or

b in acquiring an interest (other than a legal interest) in fully-paid shares in the company if no consideration is given for the acquisition by the company or an entity it controls; or

c under a court order; or

d *in circumstances covered by subsection 259B(2) or (3).'*

Under s 259F of the Act, if a contravention has occurred, a person who was involved (which is widely defined and includes any person who was, directly or indirectly, knowingly concerned in or party to the contravention) in the contravention may be subject to a civil penalty of up to $200,000. There are also potential criminal consequences that can flow from the breach.

Due to the potentially significant penalties that can arise under the

Act, together with the likely adverse commercial ramifications, any identified breach of s 259A should be remedied as soon as practical following identification of the issue.

One option is for the persons involved in the contravention to apply to ASIC for a no-action letter, whereby ASIC confirms it does not intend to take any steps as a result of a particular contravention of the Act.

As flagged above, a breach of the Act most typically arises where a trustee company of a family discretionary trust is listed under ASIC records as having its shares owned by the trust. That is, the trustee of the trust owns shares in itself. While "circular" ownership arrangements can be beneficial from an asset protection perspective, they must still comply with the Act.

The preferred approach therefore, where the shares in a corporate beneficiary are to be owned by a trust, is for a structure along the following lines:

(1) the shares in the corporate trustee should be owned by individuals with a low risk profile;
(2) the corporate trustee should undertake no activities other than its trusteeship and the value of the shares in the trustee company should therefore be limited to their issue price; and
(3) the trustee company in its capacity as trustee should own all of the shares in the corporate beneficiary.

The Richstar decision and beyond

The Richstar decision in 2006 set alarm bells ringing because of its redefinition of established discretionary trust principles.

Background

The Richstar case stemmed from the litigation surrounding the failed WestPoint group. The Federal Court had already appointed receivers to the property of several directors and companies of the failed group. ASIC sought to have the meaning of 'property' (for the purposes of it being available for distribution amongst creditors) extended to include property held by a third party on trust for a defendant, including where the defendant was a general beneficiary of a discretionary trust.

The key issue considered by the decision was the definition of 'property' in section 9 Corporations Act 2001 (**Corporations Act**). Section 9 provides that property 'means any legal or equitable estate or interest (whether present or future and whether vested or contingent) in real or personal property of any description and includes a thing in action'.

The Court held that some of the defendants had 'at least a contingent interest' in the trust property, which was sufficient for the property to be available to the receivers. A contingent interest was found to arise where 'the trustee is effectively, the alter ego of the relevant beneficiary or otherwise subject to his or its effective control'.

Although this was not the full order sought by ASIC, the decision challenged the traditional view that a beneficiary of a discretionary trust has a mere 'expectancy', which is not sufficient to constitute 'property' which is available to creditors.

The Court held that the difference between 'exhaustive' and 'non-exhaustive' discretionary trusts was important.

Exhaustive trusts

Under an 'exhaustive' trust, the trust deed requires the trustee to distribute all of the income after each defined period.

Where an exhaustive trust has a closed class of beneficiaries, the beneficiaries as a group can direct the trustee how to deal with the property, and can require that the legal interest in the property be transferred to them.

Non-exhaustive trusts

Under a 'non-exhaustive' trust deed, the trustee can distribute the trust income however they see fit whether that is a distribution of some, none or all of the trust income.

Under a non-exhaustive trust deed, even a closed class of beneficiaries acting together cannot direct the trustee how to deal with the trust property.

Richstar held that 'in the ordinary case the beneficiary of a discretionary trust, other than perhaps the sole beneficiary of an exhaustive trust, does not have an equitable interest in the trust income or property which would fall within even the most generous definition of 'property' in section 9 of the Corporations Act'.

However, the Court went on to 'distinguish the "ordinary case" from the case in which the beneficiary effectively controls the trustee's power of selection', in case, 'there is something which is akin to a proprietary interest in the beneficiary'.

Issues not considered

Somewhat surprisingly, the judgment did not address whether any of the trusts in question had default beneficiaries, even though default beneficiaries have long been regarded as perhaps having a legal interest in the trust property. Further, although some significance was given to the identity of the appointor, no mention was made of previous cases which have held that an appointor's power of appointment is not 'property' for the purposes of the Bankruptcy Act.

Effect of Richstar

On its face, the Richstar decision appears to support the position that discretionary trust assets cannot be regarded as the 'property' of a person merely because that person is a beneficiary, trustee, director or shareholder of a trustee company, or an appointor.

However, certain combinations of these roles may be sufficient to trigger a finding of effective control and hence an interest in 'property'. The distinction between the effect of each role individually and the effect of a combination of roles was not discussed in any detail in the case.

For many years, the Family Court has been able to 'look through' formal trust structures to decide who has de facto ownership of trust property.

The decision in Richstar was significant because it was the first time that a beneficiary's interest in a discretionary trust had been held to potentially amount to a form of property in a commercial situation.

The decision in Richstar considered a number of Family Court cases in concluding that it was appropriate to look beyond the structure of the different legal entities involved (including lifting the corporate veil) to determine whether the relevant person could have been said to have effective control of the assets in question, and thus some form of contingent interest.

The Court considered the likelihood that a beneficiary who controlled the trustee's power of selection would have exercised that power in their own favour. In this regard, it was held that:

> 'where a discretionary trust is controlled by a trustee who is in truth the alter ego of a beneficiary, then at the very least, a contingent interest may be identified because it is as good as certain that the beneficiary will receive the benefits of distributions either of income or capital or both.'

What does this mean for discretionary trusts?

The decision in Richstar represents a significant departure from the traditional view of discretionary trusts, but it was far from conclusive. As the case involved an interlocutory application in relation to a specific provision of the Corporations Act, its application was, and arguably still is, limited to similar fact scenarios. It is also worth remembering that this was an interim decision to preserve the trust assets held. Whether the assets could in fact be distributed to creditors, was not considered.

The main concern is that, if this approach is accepted and adopted generally within the context of appointing receivers, it could pave the way for trust assets to be available to, for example, trustees in bankruptcy or company liquidators. If this were to happen, maintaining 'control' over a trustee would come at the significant price of reduced asset protection.

Cases since Richstar

It is also important to remember that the 'Richstar decision' was only a single judge interim decision While the judge is now the Chief Justice of the High Court, the decision itself has not yet been followed or applied by any other judges and could still be challenged in the future.

Furthermore in Public Trustee v Smith[16] (Smith) there is some indication of the likely scope of the Richstar decision. The key issue in Smith was whether property that was owned by a discretionary trust could be considered as being owned by a person, who was the sole shareholder and director of the corporate trustee, to enable the assets to be gifted via that person's will.

The Court made a clear distinction between actual ownership and effective ownership and concluded that the will maker was not the actual (beneficial) owner of the trust assets. In relation to Richstar it was noted by the Court in that case:

> 'Did not say that it followed from the defendant's position as beneficiaries of discretionary trusts and their control of the trustees that this amounted to actual ownership as distinct from effective control'

In Smith, the Judge also confirmed:

> 'I do not understand ... Richstar... to establish that because a beneficiary of a discretionary trust controls the appointment or removal of the trustee, or controls the exercise of the trustee's power and can appoint trust property to himself or herself, that the holder of such a power is the beneficial owner of the trust property irrespective of the terms of the trust deed'.

The above reasoning in Smith was applied by the same judge in a subsequent 2008 case.

Conclusion

For the time being, the benefits of discretionary trusts are generally still sufficient to make them the preferred structure for asset protection purposes.

That said, the issues and questions raised in Richstar remain significant and care should be taken when restructuring and establishing discretionary trusts.

In this regard, arguably the optimal approach for the establishment or review of any trust deed is to methodically follow a tailored checklist.

An example in this regard of some of the matters that should normally be considered is set out below. The various questions summarised above in the Beeson case are also obviously relevant.

20 Point Checklist – Trust review

1	What is the vesting date for the trust, and has it passed already?
2	Should the trust deed be amended due to changes in the law since it was established?
3	Does the trust deed restrict the range of beneficiaries who can receive income or capital distributions? Is the trustee excluded from receiving distributions?
4	Can beneficiaries be removed or added?
5	What is the date by which income distributions should be made in each financial year?
6	How is trust income defined and does the trustee have power to alter the meaning of trust income?
7	Does the trustee have absolute discretion in relation to income and capital distributions?
8	Is there a default distribution of the income and capital of the trust to particular beneficiaries?
9	Does the deed deem unpaid distributions to be treated as loans by the beneficiary?

10	Who is the trustee of the trust? If the trustee ceases to act, do their powers pass to anyone else, and if so, who?
11	Does the trustee need consent/approval of any other person to exercise any of its powers?
12	Does someone (e.g. a principal, guardian, appointor) have the power to unilaterally change the trustee?
13	Is the role of trustee and principal (if any) automatically terminated on certain events (for example death or bankruptcy)?
14	If the principal ceases to act, do their powers automatically pass to anyone else, and if so, who?
15	Is the trustee in reality the 'alter ego' of an 'at risk' person?
16	Will the trust own more than one asset class?
17	Has there been a pattern of income or capital distributions to 'at risk' beneficiaries?
18	Is there a power to vary, and are there any restrictions on that power?
19	Have variations to the deed been validly made e.g. is there an appropriate exercise of the variation power and have all necessary consents been obtained?
20	What is the governing jurisdiction?

Acknowledgements

This article has been based on material prepared by each of the other directors at View Legal, Patrick Ellwood and Naomi Arnold at View Legal. The assistance of each of them is gratefully acknowledged, however all errors are my own.

Disclaimer

This article covers legal and technical issues in a general way. It is not designed to express opinions on specific cases. This article is intended for information purposes only and should not be regarded as legal advice. Further advice should be obtained before taking action on any issue dealt with in this publication.

References

[1] Richstar Enterprises Pty Ltd (ACN 099 071 968) v Carey (No 6) [2006] FCA 814

[2] *Taxation in Australia* Vol 47(10) May 2013, 646

[3] *Taxation in Australia* Vol 47(10) May 2013, 646

[4] Kennon v Spry [(2008) HCA 56]

[5] Stanford v Stanford (2012) HCA 52

[6] Beeson v Spence [2007] FamCA 200

[7] Schweitzer & Schweitzer [2012] FamCA 445

[8] MacDowell & Williams and Ors [2012] FamCA 479

[9] FCT & Darling and Anor [2013] FamCA118

[10] Williams v Lloyd [1934] HCA1

[11] Gartside v Inland Revenue Commissioners [1968] AC 553

[12] Harris v Harris [2011] FamCAFC 245

[13] Dwyer v Ross (1992) 34 FCR 463

[14] Wily v Burton (1994) 126 ALR 557

[15] Montevento Holdings Pty Ltd v Scaffidi (2012) HCA 48

[16] Public Trustee v Smith [20081 NSWCA 397]

INSURANCE FUNDED BUSINESS SUCCESSION

Insurance funded business succession

Introduction

ON 1 JULY 2014, changes to the type of total and permanent disablement (**TPD**) insurance policies which can be owned through superannuation took effect.

As TPD policies commonly feature in insurance-funded buy-sell agreements, it is timely to review the various ways these agreements can be structured.

This article provides an overview of:

a how most insurance funded buy-sell agreements operate;
b the alternatives available when determining how the insurance policies should be owned; and
c the taxation consequences of the different ownership approaches.

This article also considers the likely impact on insurance arrangements of the *Tax and Superannuation Laws Amendment (2014 Measures No. 7) Bill 2014* (**Bill**), which at the time of writing is before Parliament.

What is an insurance funded buy-sell agreement?

A buy-sell agreement is a contractual arrangement between members of a jointly owned business (for instance, a company).

The agreement is structured so that subject to certain events relating to the departure of a principal, the continuing principals are given the option, or in some cases are obliged, to purchase the interest of the departing principal.

For ease of reading, the word 'partner' is used in this article as a short hand reference to any owner, whether an individual or entity and regardless of whether the business entity is a partnership, company or trust.

Similarly, the word 'principal' is used to describe the ultimate individual behind each partner.

Why are buy-sell agreements important?

Buy-sell agreements are important for two main reasons.

First, no one is able to know when a death or a traumatic event will occur. As a result, there is often insufficient capital available for the remaining principals to buy out the exiting principal without suffering financial hardship.

Secondly, if one of the principals in a business dies, significant commercial difficulties can arise. For example, the business might continue to operate for the primary benefit of the exiting owner's family, even though others are undertaking all the work.

Further, it might be the case that the deceased principal's spouse (who is unsuited and unskilled in the running of a business) wishes to become involved in a way that could have adverse consequences on the business' financial sustainability.

The potential consequences of the unexpected exit of a principal are generally unfavourable, reinforcing the reasons why buy-sell agreements are so important for the sustainability of a business.

The types of events which are usually dealt with in a buy-sell agreement are:

a death;
b TPD; and
c trauma.

While there are a number of other events which can result in a principal exiting a business, for a combination of reasons it is often easier to deal only with insurable events under a buy-sell agreement and use a separate partnership agreement to address non-insurable triggering events.

Self-owned policies

Anecdotally the most common way to structure an insurance funded buy-sell arrangement is as follows:

a the insurance policies are self-owned by each principal;
b the arrangements between the partners are documented in a put and call option agreement;
c the quantum of insurance is reviewed regularly to ensure that it is adequate in all circumstances; and
d the purchase price under the put and call option agreement is a nominal amount (e.g. $1) plus the amount by which the market value of the interest transferred (including loans) at the date of the triggering event exceeds the insurance proceeds received by the outgoing partner. Obviously if the insurance proceeds exceed the market value of the outgoing partner's interest, then the disposal price will simply be $1.

If there is a claim made under the self-owned insurance policy, the insurance proceeds go directly to the principal who has been affected by a triggering event under the buy-sell agreement or to that principal's estate.

Once the option has been exercised, the exiting partner is deemed to have disposed of equity and interest in the partnership, at market value, to the remaining partners, who similarly acquire the interest at market value.[1]

Capital gains tax (CGT) issues - agreement

Mandatory agreements

Insurance funded buy-sell agreements normally provide that, on the death of a partner, the continuing partners can purchase, or be forced to purchase, the deceased partner's interests.

The same provisions would apply for TPD and trauma, if insurance has been obtained. In this regard, insurance funded arrangements are distinguished from other buy-sell arrangements, where it is unusual for the continuing partners to be contractually bound to purchase the retiring partner's interest, given the funding difficulties, which might arise.

Section 104-10 (CGT event A1) of the *Income Tax Assessment Act 1997* (**ITAA 1997**) (formerly section 160U(3) of the *Income Tax Assessment Act 1936* (**ITAA 1936**)) deals with the timing of disposal and acquisition of CGT assets, and provides that the contract is entered into at the time of a CGT event that involves disposal of an asset.

Historically the Australian Taxation Office (**ATO**) has argued that the entry into a buy-sell agreement obliging the continuing partners to purchase an outgoing partner's interest will amount to a disposal of that partner's interest at the time of entering into the buy-sell agreement, and not at the time the continuing partners actually acquire the outgoing partner's interest following death, TPD or trauma.[2]

While it was accepted that the consideration received for disposal of the partnership interest was determined at the time of actual transfer following the triggering event; for CGT purposes, the time of the CGT event was taken to be the date of entering into the buy-sell agreement.

For obvious reasons, many advisers in this area had considerable difficulty in accepting the historic ATO view.

In particular, section 104-10 should not be seen to apply to the buy-sell agreement; rather, it applies to the agreement created on the occurrence of a triggering event.

A buy-sell agreement does not involve any acquisition or disposal of an asset; the agreement merely records an arrangement whereby, if a triggering event occurs at some time in the future, then the continuing partners will acquire the deceased partner's interest at that time, based on a formula contained in the document.

The issue of when a contract is made involves consideration of difficult issues of contract law, and it is fair to say that the law is not entirely clear.

Buy and sell options

Due to the longstanding (and at times significant) uncertainty surrounding 'standard' buy-sell agreements, many specialists in this area structure the contractual arrangements using options.

In particular, the use of appropriately drafted put (sell) and call (buy) options essentially avoids any argument that the agreement might have been entered into at a time before the triggering event.

The use of put and call arrangements can also allow for greater flexibility in structuring the general estate planning objectives of the partners.

For example, option based arrangements mean partners might choose to dispose of their interests in the partnership on death via their wills (if this suits their objectives), thereby ensuring that no CGT or stamp duty is payable on the disposal.

This would not be the case had the disposal taken place pursuant to a mandatory buy-sell agreement.

Under a put and call option arrangement, the continuing partners have an option to acquire an interest of an outgoing partner on the occurrence of a triggering event (**call or buy option**), and the outgoing partner has an option to sell the partnership interest to the continuing partners for a specified time after the triggering event (**put or sell option**).

The granting of an option constitutes the acquisition of a CGT asset by the grantee, pursuant to section 109-5 but is not otherwise a

CGT event for the grantee. For the grantor, CGT event D2 will be triggered when the option is granted.

In both instances, as there is usually no payment for the granting of the option and the market value is essentially nil, there should be no CGT consequences upon execution of a buy sell agreement containing either or both a put or call option. These outcomes have been confirmed by the ATO in its withdrawn Discussion Paper.[3]

A variation on the put and call option arrangements is simply to hold unexecuted contracts in escrow until the predetermined triggering event takes place; this approach, however, is less common than the put and call option agreement.

Deemed market value substitution rule

It is generally accepted that where a business succession plan is structured with self-owned insurance policies and a buy-sell deed using put and call options, the deemed market value substitution rules apply for taxation purposes.4

As a result, the seller is deemed to have received market value for their interest and the buyer receives a market value cost base for their acquisition.

This outcome occurs notwithstanding that the transfer has been funded (either wholly or partly) by insurance.

ATO Discussion Paper

It should be noted that the ATO has withdrawn its insurance funded business succession Discussion Paper.

As a result, in its December 2010 minutes, the National Tax Liaison Group (**NTLG**) stated that the ATO had confirmed that the withdrawn Discussion Paper should not be relied on and that members should instruct practitioners to refrain from relying on the Discussion Paper.[5]

This said, the Discussion Paper remains the only substantive document released by the ATO in this area and, despite its withdrawal, is often referenced as a potentially indicative guide on many of the relevant principles.

For example, the application of section 104-10 to buy-sell arrangements is dealt with in some detail in the ATO's Discussion Paper.

Despite years of suggesting the contrary, the ATO appears to accept that where an agreement is clearly drafted on the basis that it is not to come into effect until after a triggering event, then the time of disposal will be delayed until the triggering event.

In the Discussion Paper, the ATO places significant emphasis on the distinction between conditions precedent to formation of the contract and conditions precedent to performance of the contract (also referred to as conditions subsequent).

To determine which type of condition precedent applies, the ATO suggests there must be an examination of whether the parties to the buy-sell agreement are bound by the agreement (meaning there is no doubt that, at some time in the future, there will be a disposal of an interest pursuant to the buy-sell agreement).

If this is the case, then a triggering event will be a condition precedent to performance of obligations of the parties (not to formation of the agreement) and the relevant date under section 104-10 will be the date on which the agreement is entered into.

If the parties are able to dispose of their interest in the partnership before the triggering event occurs, then the ATO concludes that such an agreement is not certain and the time of the CGT event for section 104-10 purposes will be the occurrence of the triggering event. In other words, there is a condition precedent to the actual formation of the agreement.

Thus, the intention of the parties to delay the disposal date of their interests should be clearly set out in the buy-sell agreement. Commercially, the easiest way to document the intention is well structured options.

CGT issues - insurance policies

Life insurance

Section 118-300 ITAA 1997 provides that the proceeds received on disposal of a life insurance policy (e.g. on the death of the life assured or on surrender of the policy) are exempt from CGT. This exemption however, is only available to:

a the original beneficial owner of the policy; and
b an assignee of the policy who did not acquire the rights or interest in the policy for an amount of money or other consideration.

This section has also led to some uncertainty in the structuring of life insurance policies supporting buy-sell arrangements, and a number of variations have developed. The major difficulty arises where there is change in the constitution of a partnership, particularly when new members join the partnership.

Incoming partners who acquire an interest in existing life insurance policies are not 'original beneficial owners'. Furthermore, it is arguable that the incoming partners do in fact pay 'an amount of money or other consideration' in acquiring their interest in the policy.

TPD and trauma insurance

Section 118-37 ITAA 1997 contains a CGT exemption for non-death insurance benefits, including TPD and trauma insurance.

The exemption applies to 'compensation or damages you receive for any wrong, injury or illness you or your relative suffers personally'.

'Relative' is defined as a person's spouse, parent, grandparent, brother, sister, uncle, aunt, nephew, niece, lineal descendant or adopted child, and those people's respective spouses.[6]

Consequently this has meant the conservative approach was that TPD or trauma proceeds were only exempt from CGT where they are received by the injured person or their relative.

This position is subject to the amendments contained in the Bill, discussed later in this article.

Superannuation (including SMSF) policy ownership

For many years, the ownership of insurance policies for buy-sell arrangements through a self-managed superannuation fund (**SMSF**) – or, for that matter, corporate funds - has been popular, at least anecdotally.

The primary advantages of policy ownership via superannuation being utilised to fund buy-sell arrangements include:

a the premiums in relation to the insurance policies are normally deductible, 'freeing up' money outside the superannuation environment that would otherwise be needed to fund insurance premiums;
b the insurance proceeds can often be utilised within the superannuation fund to generate tax effective income streams via pensions; and
c binding death benefit nominations (whether lapsing or non-lapsing) can be used to ensure that the proceeds from the policy pass as intended by the exiting partner.

In deciding whether or not to structure insurance ownership through superannuation, there are numerous issues that need to be considered, including:

a the impact of contribution limits, which can significantly undermine the usefulness of the strategy in many situations;
b the possibility that CGT might be payable on any component of an insurance payout in relation to trauma or TPD;
c whether there are circumstances surrounding the structure, which might jeopardise the ability of the superannuation fund to satisfy the sole purpose test, set out under the superannuation legislation;[7] and
d whether the arrangements are likely to fall foul of the general anti-avoidance provisions under Part IVA of the ITAA 1936.[8]

Historically the ATO has confirmed in various private documents that, when structured appropriately, a superannuation fund can own an insurance policy designed to assist the funding of a buy-sell arrangement, without breaching any tax or superannuation laws. While some organisations and specialists have received confirmation from the ATO in this area, there are no publically available statements at least in relation to industry funds.

In relation to self managed superannuation funds the ATO has indicated that there may be difficulties in satisfying the sole purpose test, presumably where the fund has few if any other investments of activities.[9]

It should also be remembered that there is the ongoing risk that some form of cap (not dissimilar to the former 'reasonable benefit limit' system) will be imposed on withdrawals from superannuation.

July 2014 changes

Best practice often dictates that clients should obtain TPD insurance protection on the basis of their inability to work in their 'own' occupation, as opposed to 'any' occupation.

The satisfaction of the 'own' occupation test is obviously easier than the condition of release set out under the superannuation legislation, that is, that a member must be incapable of working in 'any' occupation.

For a number of years, where 'own' occupation TPD insurance was owned via superannuation there was a risk that the fund may not be able to release an insurance payout to the member until some other condition of release was satisfied (for example, reaching the retirement age).

In addition, the deductibility of premiums for 'own' occupation TPD insurance has been a point of contention. From 1 July 2011, 'own' occupation premiums were only deductible to the extent the policy was attributable to 'any' occupation cover.[10]

From 1 July 2014, legislative amendments prohibit the acquisition of 'own' occupation TPD policies through superannuation.[11] These changes also effectively prohibit ownership of trauma policies via superannuation.

Existing policies can however be maintained under grandfathering arrangements.

Cross-owned insurance arrangements between partners

Cross-owned insurance is an arrangement where each partner has a fractional interest in the policies on the lives of other partners.

Specifically, partners join together to take out an insurance policy on all partners, other than themselves.

The beneficiaries of each cross-owned insurance policy are the other partners. Upon the death of any partner, the continuing partners use the insurance proceeds to purchase the interest of the deceased partner.

Under cross-owned policy ownership, a CGT exemption normally applies in relation to death benefits, but non-death benefits (i.e. TPD and trauma) usually incur CGT liability due to the interaction of sections 118-300 and 118-37(1)(b) ITAA 1997.

In particular, while section 118-300 generally exempts any life policy proceeds as long as they are received by the original beneficial owner of the policy (regardless of who that owner might be), as outlined above section 118-37(1)(b) only exempts non life insurance proceeds if they are received by the injured person or their relative.

In addition to the CGT consequences of cross-ownership, the structure also has a number of practical difficulties associated with it:

a having received the proceeds of the policy following another partner suffering a triggering event, a continuing partner may decide to start up a new business. This ultimately leaves the estate of the exiting partner with no insurance proceeds and an interest in a non-existent business;
b if the partnership dissolves it is not possible for partners to take their respective policies, as they do not in fact own them. This

can cause significant problems, particularly where one, or more, of the partners becomes uninsurable after the original policy has been acquired; and

c cross-owned insurance allows few, if any, planning opportunities following a triggering event; a formal disposal must always take place because the continuing partner has the proceeds of the insurance, while the estate of the exiting partner retains an interest in the business.

For these reasons, specialists rarely recommend cross-ownership for buy-sell arrangements and most historical cross-owned arrangements only remain in place where there are prohibitive costs in restructuring the existing arrangements.

Insurance via a special purpose trust

The use of a trust ownership model to facilitate policy ownership and the legal framework of the buy-sell agreement is the final substantive approach to be considered.

While there is a significant amount of industry literature in relation to the trust ownership model, unfortunately, as with many other aspects of insurance funded arrangements, the ATO's position has until the release of the Bill been somewhat unclear.

The trust ownership approach generally involves the establishment of a special purpose entity, often with an independent trustee company appointed to acquire the insurance policies and then distribute proceeds, on the exit of a partner, in accordance with the terms of the trust instrument.

If the trading entity is itself a trust or owned via a trust (for example, a discretionary trust owning shares in a trading company), then it may not be necessary to establish a separate structure.

The core benefit of an insurance trust is often its ability to centralise the ownership of all insurance policies and facilitate the efficient transition of a partnership interest following a triggering event.

However, many of the practical issues related to cross ownership, outlined above, also have an impact on a trust ownership model. Given that with the trust ownership model superannuation ownership is impossible, the disadvantages often seem to outweigh the potential advantages.

Historically, from a tax perspective, the level of uncertainty (compared with that of other ownership models outlined above) has undermined the trust ownership approach.

If an insurance policy is taken out by a trustee (who is also the beneficiary of the policy) over the partners of the business, proceeds paid directly to the trustee are likely to be exempt from CGT pursuant to section 118-300 ITAA 1997.

However, due to a lack of guidance from the ATO many advisers believed the same CGT problems, as summarised in relation to cross-owned insurance above, were likely to apply where there is an addition of a partner to the trustee or insurance policy.

Assuming the Bill (discussed in more detail below) is passed as currently drafted, most of the previous tax related concerns with trust ownership will be addressed.

ATO ruling

The ATO has released a Product Ruling (PR2010/18) in relation to the CGT consequences for the beneficiary of what is generally seen as a 'standard' insurance trust deed.

In many respects, the ruling reflects what most specialists in this area have advised for many years, namely that a properly crafted insurance trust deed should provide appropriate protection for the principals of a business without any significant tax detriment, notwithstanding that there might be other commercial issues to consider regarding the structure.

Unfortunately, the positive aspects of the ruling are largely undermined by the fact that the outcomes are based on the assumption that the insurance trust deed will in fact create absolute entitlement for each beneficiary in the relevant insurance policy. [12]

The expressed views of the ATO concerning absolute entitlement are, however, somewhat contentious and the ATO continues to refer to a draft ruling that has never been finalised – despite being issued in 2004.[13] The Bill addresses these issues, as summarised below.

One practical issue in this regard is that the Product Ruling confirms that, in order to ensure absolute entitlement, the relevant beneficiary must be able to call for the asset at any time. This largely undermines one of the main commercial reasons why advisers have historically recommended insurance trusts, being that the trustee will be able to control the payment of any insurance proceeds received.

A further practical issue, given the way in which many providers have traditionally structured trust arrangements, is that the Product Ruling only relates to insurance trust deeds where the company acting as trustee is an entity owned and controlled by the principals involved in the business entity and the relevant insurer is not a party to the arrangements.

ATO ruling

Minutes released from a National Tax Liaison Group meeting in 2010 provide further insight into the ATO views in relation to insurance trust deeds.[14]

In summary the minutes state:

a the status of taxation ruling on absolute entitlement (TR2004/D25) remains unclear;

b the ATO considers the finalisation of TR2004/D25 as intricately linked to how it will deal with bare trusts, which again remains an unresolved issue;

c the ATO confirms that the product ruling released by the ATO in relation to one provider's insurance trust arrangement is based entirely on the assumption that absolute entitlement was created. This assumption might be an unwise one to make, given the ATO's apparent attitude in this area; and

d. while the ATO flags that they will further consider providing appropriate guidance, they specifically confirm that the 2000 ATO Discussion Paper, on business succession arrangements, cannot be considered current (as set out above).

Traditionally the ATO has adopted a very narrow interpretation as to what in fact constitutes a bare trust. This narrow approach was confirmed by the ATO in the yet to be finalised, Taxation Ruling 2004/D25.

Ultimately, given the complexities in this area and the uncertainty created by the ATO Discussion Paper, TR 2004/D25, and the Product Ruling, many advisers have traditionally recommended obtaining a private ruling on any proposed trust arrangement documenting an insurance funded buy sell agreement from the ATO before implementing the strategy. Again, this issue is addressed by the Bill.

Company owned business succession insurance

A number of issues arise where a trading company obtains insurance policies for death, TDP and trauma over each of the core principals who also control the ownership of the shares in the company.

Two of the most important issues are: the tax consequences of receipt by the company of the insurance proceeds and how, practically, the transfer of shares to the surviving principals will take place.

For commercial and tax planning (particularly Division 7A) reasons, company ownership of business succession insurance can be attractive, but the disadvantages normally outweigh the benefits.

For example, on receipt of the insurance pay out by the company, further steps need to be taken to:

a. have the funds transferred to the exiting shareholders or their estates; and
b. ensure that the exiting shareholders transfer their shares.

There are other specific concerns, generally applicable to insurance policies that are intended for business succession arrangements and owned by a trading company including:

a while CGT should not be payable on receipt of life insurance proceeds, it will be payable on any TPD or trauma proceeds that are paid to a company. In contrast, no CGT should be payable on receipt of the insurance proceeds where the policies are self-owned;
b there can be significant practical difficulties in accessing insurance proceeds from a company to the appropriate recipient. This is particularly important when the main purpose of the policy is for an equity payment, as opposed to debt cover; and
c where insurance proceeds need to be accessed by the exiting principal (or the principal's estate) this is usually only achievable via a share buyback or dividend. Generally speaking, both alternatives will have inefficient tax outcomes, at least compared to an individual or trust disposing a capital asset.

Proposed changes

The Bill was introduced to the House of Representatives in December 2014 and is expected to be passed by both houses of Parliament.

Amongst other changes, the Bill amends the way insurance payments are taxed in certain circumstances.

In particular, if passed, the Bill will amend ITAA 1997 to:

a remove the requirement that, in order to access the exemption under section 118-300, the insurance proceeds are received by the original 'beneficial' owner of the life insurance policy. The amendment removes the reference to 'beneficial' to clarify that a trustee is eligible for the exemption, where they hold the beneficial interest in the policy for a beneficiary;
b extend the exemption for compensation for injury/illness (i.e. TPD/trauma insurance proceeds) in section 118-37 to apply

where the proceeds are received by the trustee of a trust or superannuation fund (subject to the policy ownership prohibitions outlined above), if the injured/ill person is a beneficiary of the trust; and

c insert a CGT exemption where a trustee makes a payment to a beneficiary (or their legal personal representative) in respect of life, TPD or trauma insurance proceeds. This change also ensures that where the relevant trust is a unit trust, CGT event E4 does not apply.

The proposed amendments appear likely to make trust and superannuation fund ownership of life, TPD or trauma insurance policies more attractive in some circumstances, given the new clarity regarding the tax treatment of the insurance proceeds.

Importantly, the Bill also confirms that as the changes reflect the intended administrative position, they will apply from 1 July 2005 and taxpayers adversely impacted who would otherwise be out of time will be granted an extension to amend their returns.

Taxation Determinations

The CGT Cell of the ATO has issued a series of Taxation Determinations concerning different aspects of section 118-300 ITAA 1997 that are relevant in the context of buy-sell arrangements.

A summary of the conclusions reached in each Determination is outlined briefly below.

TD94/31

The original beneficial owner is the person who first takes out the policy and holds the policy in their own right and for their own benefit.

Where a trustee takes out a life insurance policy on behalf of beneficiaries of a trust, the trustee is not the original beneficial owner.

Thus, if the trustee pays an amount of money or other consideration to acquire the rights under the policy, then the trustee would be subject to CGT on the proceeds received on disposal of the rights under the policy unless:

a item 5 of the table at section 118-300 ITAA 1997 applies (in other words policies are owned via complying superannuation funds); or
b the trustee is a bare trustee that is, there is a beneficiary who is absolutely entitled to the rights under the policy as against the trustees (in which case section 106-50 deems the disposal to be by the beneficiary).

For completeness, this determination is likely to be amended or revoked if the Bill passes, in light of the amendments to section 118-300.

TD94/32

Section 112-20 will not apply to deem a market value consideration for section 118-300 ITAA 1997 purposes where no amount of money or consideration is given for the acquisition of rights under a life insurance policy.

TD94/33

The exemption from CGT on disposal of a life insurance policy under section 118-300 ITAA 1997 is available on any disposal of the policy by an original beneficial owner, and not just in the specific instances mentioned in section 118-300. Again, the Bill is likely to see this determination amended or revoked.

TD94/34

Where an assignment of rights under, or an interest in, a policy is made by way of gift (and therefore no money or other consideration is given) then payment of the ongoing premiums by the assignee will not be taken to be amounts of money paid to acquire those rights or interest so as to deny the CGT.

Therefore, the CGT exemption provided by section 118-300 ITAA 1997 will remain available.

Conclusion

Succession planning is a critical issue for any jointly owned business.

The unexpected exit of a principal can result in a range of adverse ramifications for the profitability (and potentially the ongoing viability) of a business together with unintended revenue consequences, however appropriate structured insurance funding can be an important step in mitigating these risks.

Acknowledgement

The authors gratefully acknowledge the assistance of the directors and staff at View Legal in the preparation of the paper, particularly Naomi Arnold.

References

1 Pursuant to the market value substitution rule in sections 116-30 and 112-20 *Income Tax Assessment Act 1997* (Cth).

2 ATO, *Discussion Paper in relation to Buy-Sell (business concession) agreements.*

3 Ibid p 9.

4 Sections 116-30 and 112-20 *Income Tax Assessment Act 1997* (Cth).

5 NTLG December 2010 minutes at item 9.

6 Defined in section 995-1 *Income Tax Assessment Act 1997* (Cth).

7 Section 62 *Superannuation Industry (Supervision) Act* 1993 (Cth).

8 Sections 177-A to 177-G *Income Tax Assessment Act* 1936 (Cth).

9 ATO SMSF News – edition 30 – Maintaining the integrity of the SMSF sector

10 Pursuant to regulation 295-465.01.

11 *Superannuation Industry (Supervision) Regulation (SISR)* 4.07D.

12 PR2010/18 at paragraph 4

13 See Taxation Ruling TR 2004/D25 'Income tax: capital gains: meaning of the words 'absolutely entitled to a CGT asset as against the trustee of a trust'

14 NTLG December 2010 minutes, item 9

Printed in Dunstable, United Kingdom

91343653R00157